WHIPPED

BY CAROL QUEEN

The Leather Daddy and the Femme: An Erotic Novel

Exhibitionism for the Shy: Show Off, Dress Up and Talk Hot

Real Live Nude Girl: Chronicles of Sex-Positive Culture

EDITED BY CAROL QUEEN

Five-Minute Erotica: 35 Passionate Tales of Sex and Seduction

Best Bisexual Erotica (with Bill Brent)

Best Bisexual Erotica, Volume 2 (with Bill Brent)

PoMoSexuals: Challenging Assumptions About Gender and Sexual-

ity

(with Lawrence Schimel)

Switch Hitters: Lesbians Write Gay Male Erotica and Gay Men

Write Lesbian Erotica (with Lawrence Schimel)

Sex Spoken Here: Good Vibrations Erotic Reading Circle Selections

(with Jack Davis)

WHIPPED

20 EROTIC STORIES of FEMALE DOMINANCE

EDITED BY
Carol Queen

CHAMBERLAIN BROS.

A MEMBER OF PENGUIN GROUP (USA) INC.

NEW YORK

CHAMBERLAIN BROS.
Published by the Penguin Group
Penguin Group (USA) Inc., 375 Hudson Street, New York, New York 10014, USA • Penguin
Group (Canada), 90 Eglinton Avenue East, Suite 700, Toronto, Ontario M4P 2Y3, Canada
(a division of Pearson Penguin Canada Inc.) • Penguin Books Ltd, 80 Strand, London WC2R
0RL, England • Penguin Ireland, 25 St Stephen's Green, Dublin 2, Ireland (a division of Pen-
guin Books Ltd) • Penguin Group (Australia), 250 Camberwell Road, Camberwell, Victoria
3124, Australia (a division of Pearson Australia Group Pty Ltd) • Penguin Books India Pvt Ltd,
11 Community Centre, Panchsheel Park, New Delhi–110 017, India • Penguin Group (NZ),
Cnr Airborne and Rosedale Roads, Albany, Auckland 1310, New Zealand (a division of Pearson
New Zealand Ltd) • Penguin Books (South Africa) (Pty) Ltd, 24 Sturdee Avenue, Rosebank,
Johannesburg 2196, South Africa

Penguin Books Ltd, Registered Offices: 80 Strand, London WC2R 0RL, England

LIBRARY OF CONGRESS CATALOGING-IN-PUBLICATION DATA

Whipped : 20 erotic stories of female dominance/edited by Carol Queen.
    p.   cm.
    ISBN 1-59609-046-4
    1. Erotic stories, American.   2. Sexual dominance and submission—Fiction.   I. Queen,
Carol.
PS648.E7W49   2005   2005045506
813'.01083538—dc22

Printed in the United States of America
10 9 8 7 6 5 4 3 2 1

Book design by Jaime Putorti

Contents

CONTENTS

Introduction

The writers, mistresses, and scene players gathered together in *Whipped* know something about the farther shores of pleasure, means of transgression and transcendence that take what you think you know about the erotic and twist it into beautiful and frightening new shapes. Though many people—more than you would ever guess—are hot for power play, role-playing, fetish, and the whole complex tangle of pleasures we sometimes shorten to BDSM, these tale-tellers specialize in what happens when women take the reins of power. And whether they're telling you their own tales of transformative dominance and submission or searing top/bottom erotic play, or spinning out their (or perhaps your) fantasies, they want to give you more space to both live and fantasize.

1

There's no telling what lurks in the dark corners of one's erotic psyche; many of us don't even know our most hidden sexual dreams until we stumble into a relationship with someone who knows how to draw them out of us. Or we surf the net for a new kind of porn and find ourselves in the grip of a fantasy we didn't know we had. The same thing can happen browsing a book . . . like this one.

Or maybe you're reading just to find out what this dominant/submissive stuff is all about. Together with *Whipped!*, the video, you will learn a lot in these pages, for I have tried to choose a wide range of stories and true personal tales to entice, yes, but also to inform. Erotic play like this is misunderstood. And while you'll find whips and chains here, you'll find many other things, too . . . sexual dominance, mistresses (professional and lifestyle alike) who play fast and loose with gender roles or sexual orientation, the high of public exhibitionism, and the depths of emotion a submissive can feel for his or her mistress. I bet every reader will find something eye-opening here, plus something to make their pulse race. People are attracted to BDSM because it's exciting, powerful, and unexpected. Perhaps, while you turn these pages, the unexpected will happen to you.

So whether you know your own kinks through and through or are in the scary, exhilarating process of exploration and discovery, welcome to a world where women rule—at least for the night. There are no glass ceilings among the stern, voracious, confident (mostly), powerful women who take charge in the stories and memoirs in *Whipped*. And whether they want to be on top sexually or coolly mete out well-deserved punishment, they make all our erotic worlds a little bigger, and a lot more exciting.

I Am Your Kitten

BIANCA JAMES

I am a kitten. I am *your* kitten, Mistress Marthe, hiding under the bed with just the tips of my pink-polished toes peeking out, giggling to myself as you search the apartment, calling my name: *Mittens, Mittens, wherever can you be?*

Normally I'd come crawling across the carpet to welcome you home, rub my face against your stocking-clad legs and purr, waiting for you to stroke my head with your manicured hand, but today I feel like hiding. You're going to be very angry with me, I know. I want you to be a little mad. A lot mad. I'm in one of those moods.

I like the view from under the bed: the strong muscles of your calves flexing in their tall heels as you pace around the room. I crane my neck as you pass by, trying to sneak a peek up your skirt. For a moment it seems as though you've given up, and I'm dumb enough to think I've fooled you, until you drag me out from under the bed by my ankle, carpet burn scorching my delicate skin worse than any flogger could.

"Bad kitty!" you scold me, as the paddle comes down on my backside for the umpteenth time. You've brought out the paddle you save for when you're really angry—pink leather with heart-shaped cutouts that make a whooshing sound as the paddle comes down on my ass. Bent over your bed, with my tearstained face buried in a pillow that smells of your perfume, naked ass thrust in the air, legs propped up in black vinyl shoes with six-inch heels that are a little too big for my feet.

They were your favorite shoes once, now they're mine. I peed in them as revenge for the time you left me tied up in your clothes closet while you took Alice as your date to a fetish ball. You made me drink a full glass of the same piss as punishment. You threw the shoes in the trash where you thought I wouldn't find them, but I'm not too proud to go digging through the trash now and again. The odor of piss has gone faint, but I treasure these shoes more than anything, because they are the only item of clothing you've allowed me to own, apart from the pink kitten ears that I never take off, not even when I leave the house. No fancy corsets or leather garments for me. You'd have me the way God made me, curled up naked on the velvet couch or the plush carpet, fastidiously clean.

Sometimes when you're away I curl up with the shoes and just stroke them, fascinated by my own reflection in the shiny black vinyl. Never licking or chewing them, no, that would be too doggylike. But my deeply ingrained feline vanity can't resist the allure of a reflective surface.

Fifty whacks and then you have me stand in front of the mirror so we can both admire your workmanship—two crisply defined white hearts perfectly centered on bright pink ass cheeks. But no sooner have you doled out your punishment than I am splayed with my belly across your lap, as, cooing, you apply ice to the hot swollen flesh on my ass. I'm too cute for you to stay angry for long.

I am your kitten, Mistress Marthe, that is all. You keep me around because I'm cute and soft and amusing. I have no delusions that there is anything more to it. I am not your only slave, though my vanity would have me believe that I am your best-loved pet. You say you don't play favorites, but I've seen the others and none of them are as beautiful or cuddly as I am. Take middle-aged Pierre, who comes around in the maid costume and ball gag to vacuum and dust three nights a week. The rest of the time Pierre is the president of a big company, with a wife and kids, but to you he's just a worthless little worm—yes, I've heard you call him this to his face while you spanked him! All day long his underpaid immigrant maid slaves at minimum wage to clean up his family's messes, and meanwhile he pays for the privilege of touching your dirt! I have no sympathy for stupid humans like Pierre. I hate the sound of his vacuum, forcing me to squeeze into the tiny space beneath the couch like a dust-bunny and meow piteously until he is finished. He used to try to lure me out with candy, but he learned his lesson the time I hissed and scratched him with my freshly sharpened claws. You forced me to apologize for leaving marks, but I think he liked the pain.

And then there is poor little Alice, Alice with the frizzy hair and the dark circles under her eyes and a terminal sense of dread, always waiting for the next blow to fall. Alice is a poor abused secretary at an advertising agency downtown. Alice hates her job, but instead of quitting like an intelligent human would, she gives you money so you can make her feel better. Alice is such a pathetic little pain junkie, I've seen the way she begs for mercy, but she's never used her safe word, not once. I like to hide in the corner and watch while Alice is tied to the cross and you torment her with the baby pizza cutter tool, or the crackling ultraviolet wand. Alice screeches all the while, but she'd only screech louder if you stopped. And the look of terror she gets when you enter the room wearing the ten-inch strap-on is nothing compared to her sense of horror when she realizes I've been spying on her ritual humiliation for my own amusement. Alice doesn't like me, she's told you as much many times. Fair enough, I don't like her either. But I've noticed that you neglect to lock the dungeon door when you're in there playing with her, and you never forget with the others. And though you might give me an obligatory scolding, you and I both know that I'll be back. So whose cruelty runs deeper? Yours or mine?

I know that I am better than Alice and Pierre, even if you would never openly acknowledge such a truth. They are slaves, driven by their insatiable desire for pain and humiliation. Me, I maintain my pride always, even when you have to tie me up with vinyl tape just to give me a bath. I am not a slave like the others, I am your pet, and I am only your pet because I allow you the privilege of caring for me, feeding me, and playing with me. I had a reputation as a beautiful young brat before I met you, stretching the patience and inciting the wrath of a

dozen male doms, secretly getting off on their frustration at
how badly they wanted me and how uncooperative I was. These
men were insecure amateurs compared to you, Mistress Marthe.
I could have played this game well into my twenties for my
own amusement, taking pride in my sadistic streak, well
hidden beneath the innocent blue eyes and cherry lips. But
only you knew how to bring out the kitten in me, permitting
me to indulge both sides of my nature. You knew just the right
words to tame me and keep me happy while letting the wild
creature in my heart run free. It is because I adore you that I
can fall asleep with my head on your lap as you caress my hair
and watch TV. When you bring me sashimi and ice cream for
dinner, or a fuzzy heart-shaped pillow for my kitty bed, I know
you love me, too, as only a mistress can love her kitten. I love to
bring you tributes—not mauled mice or birds, but cute, innocent girls and boys handpicked from my human sexuality seminar at the university, fresh meat for you and me to play with.

You saw through to my true nature, Mistress Marthe, pen-
etrated past the layers of sweet girl flesh to the rottenness of my
very core. But it's already been a year that we've lived together,
and I can't help but wonder what will become of me when I become a full-grown cat. Will you still think I'm cute and dote
on me? Will you let me get away with humping the armrests of
the chairs in the house to mark my territory? Will you still let
me nibble your fingers as you feed me sushi with my head in
your lap, when my teeth have grown into proper fangs? Both
you and I know that I grow stronger every day, and before long
my love bites might leave permanent damage. How much
longer before I grow bored of spending lazy afternoons sleep-

ing on the couch, and start sneaking out of the house to mate with horny tomcats on rooftops?

You knew all of these things, Mistress Marthe, and so on the morning of my twenty-first birthday you presented me with two packages, luxurious boxes wrapped in tissue and carefully knotted string. I knew something was up when I opened the first box, because it contained clothes. A black vinyl catsuit, to be exact, perfectly matched to my favorite shoes. The suit must have been custom made to my measurements, because it fit my body like a second skin, with zippers placed in strategic areas. The best part, of course, was the hood, with its perky little black vinyl ears. The second package contained a toy of the sort I have never been allowed to play with before—a cat o' nine tails, the leather stiff and tight, not yet broken in. I held my breath as I touched the whip in its nest of tissue paper, as if it were a viper that might bite me. I winced a little as I held it out to you, baring my back for your ministrations. You shook your head no.

"For a year you have served as my faithful kitten," you say. "And I wish you could stay my kitten forever. But I would be a fool to ignore your fangs and claws. From this day forward, I shall no longer call you Mittens my kitten, but Gloves my apprentice."

My eyes widened with amazement—I never dreamed in nine lifetimes that you would grant me the privilege that many a wannabe domme would kill for, a gift that will be in many ways much more difficult than simply submitting to you, but far more rewarding as well.

"I never really believed you were a sub to begin with," you told me with a chuckle, causing me to blush. "But it was fun to pretend. Now, shall we go hunting for some fresh meat, my kitten?"

"But . . . didn't you just say . . ."

"Yes, but you will always be a kitten in my eyes. Nobody else has to know."

Becoming the Goddess

Carol Queen

*T*oday I am a goddess: I have access to an awesome wellspring of sexual power, I know I am beautiful, and I understand exactly why someone would desire to deliver her- or himself into my hands to say, as my very first slave did, "Anything to please you, Mistress."

But I have not always been this way. I know only a few women who seem born to their own power, with the ability to control and master appearing in them so early that it shocks everyone around them. Like my friend J, who tied up little boys when she was seven years old—and charged them a dollar to do it! A born domme.

But if anything, I was the other kind. I remember so clearly the bitter taste of lying in my lover's arms, wishing she would take control of me, push me through the intensity of her desire into a place where nothing existed but her strength and my need to serve her. But she was too afraid. And for many years so was I.

I was shy, in fact, especially sexually, as so many women are trained to be. I compensated as best I could, first by becoming an academic in control of dry information. Still, I burned to bring the knowledge to life so I could teach and inspire others. Before my life's path led me to devote myself to sexuality, I researched the goddess—whom I so needed, yet who so eluded me.

I arranged to give a lecture at the university: "Discovering the Great Goddess." It was listed in the paper. A week before it was to be held, my phone rang.

"Ms. Queen," the voice began. "What an extraordinary name. I am so intrigued by the topic of your speech next week. I have only recently moved to the area and I have been on this quest myself."

I thought perhaps I had here an overly friendly Pagan man wanting to connect with others like himself. If so, I could refer him to two or three circles whose members might let him come along to their next full moon ceremony, honoring the Great Mother at the height of her power. Maybe he could find himself a coven.

But Steve had another sort of worship in mind.

He could not have been more polite. Yet it became clear that he was inviting me to do things sexual—things I did not do, especially from the top. I knew enough about SM to know what Steve was proposing; he asked to come and serve me. In fact, by the phone call's end, he begged me.

Perhaps some women, faced with a willing submissive, can blossom immediately into their power. What kept me on the line with him did not seem to be that kind of awakening. Instead, though I did not say so, I burned with compassion for him. He had moved to this college town from San Francisco. He had left his mistress behind. He could find absolutely no community to embrace him—there was no Internet yet, and while today there is a thriving little SM club in that small city, the year I met Steve it had not yet been formed.

I did not want Steve to come and worship me. But I was alone; the woman to whom I had so yearned to give my whole soul had stopped touching me, and we had parted. I didn't draw the line at fucking men, but that didn't matter, because Steve had not called wanting to fuck.

I told him to come to my lecture and after it was over to introduce himself to me.

I knew something about SM, but not enough to anticipate Steve in the flesh. Now I know how many men like him seethe with desire no outsider could ever recognize. But that day I was surprised when he approached me: I still imagined some willowy Pagan man, an eternal boy in search of the cosmic Mother. What I got instead was an ex-Marine with a devil dog tattooed on his bicep and, despite a deferent and deeply polite manner, a scary, bearded visage. Though not tall, he had a back muscled enough to strain the fabric of his T-shirt. He looked like a biker. But he whispered as he shook my hand, "Please, Mistress. Please let me serve you."

Thinking back to it, I wonder if I had ever empathized with a man before. Looking into his eyes, I felt no fear, but I was still not sure I knew how to give him what he was seeking. I told him to come to my house the next day.

He could not hide his elation.

"What should I wear, Mistress?"

I told him to wear what his old mistress would have chosen to see him wearing.

If you had passed my curtainless house the next day, situated on a bosky side street in the town, you would have seen me sitting in my big red leather armchair with my feet extended so a powerfully built man wearing ruffled panties could rub them. I had already sent him to the bathroom to wash my lingerie. I wasn't sure what kind of slave he was, but surely holding a handful of a lesbian academic's dirty panties would be a bit of a thrill.

Then, while he rubbed my feet, I ordered him to amuse me by telling me stories of his San Francisco adventures. I often wonder today whether his mistress—I never asked her name—is one of the strong and beautiful women I now count among my dear friends. Surely all the dominas I know are capable of such blessed cruelties as he described that day.

"What was your favorite scene?"

"Mistress had a cabin in Tahoe and she ordered me to meet her there. It's a several-hour drive, through Sacramento, and she ordered me to wear these panties I am wearing for you now . . ."

He hesitated expectantly, so I said, "Yes, those panties are lovely." I suppose it might have been better to say, "How humiliating!" But if this little bear of a man had first burned with shame being made to put on rhumba panties—and pink ones, at that—he did not show it now. Because they were his link to his absent mistress, he wore them proudly.

"Go on, Steven."

"Oh, the panties were nothing, compared to what else she ordered me to do! She wanted complete dominion over my cock. She would not let me touch it. Not even to pee! She said until I came to her, the only thing that could touch my cock was her panties."

Ooooh! Nice touch, mystery mistress! This of course had Steve thinking of nothing but his cock . . . and her.

"It had already been a week. Every day I got up and put the panties on after my shower. I peed in the shower at home. That was easy. I wasn't allowed to masturbate or even scratch my balls, but peeing away from home was hardest. At work she allowed me to pee sitting down." He blushed a little at this, as if this level of feminization got to him, an old Marine, in a way the panties did not.

"But on the trip she told me not to do that. She gave me two choices. I was only allowed to use the urinal in the men's room . . ."

Oh, the truckers would love that, I bet—a tough guy carefully pulling down his pink ruffles, carefully practicing his no-hands aim. (Of course, this was long before I got my own ex-trucker, who used to wear panties all the time. This is a useful lesson about humanity: You never know for sure what kind of underwear someone has on, unless you have the opportunity to check.)

"What was your other choice?"

He blushed again. "Mistress told me I was allowed to stop the car and pee outside."

Sweet! Humiliation, cross-dressing, and exhibitionism, not to mention the extreme focus of sexual deprivation. And I had racked my brain to come up with the panty-washing idea.

"And what did you finally do?"

Steve spoke earnestly. This dilemma had clearly gripped him, and its erotic effect would be with him forever. "Well, first, I just tried not to pee at all. But she had ordered me to drink soda while I drove, and the pressure got to be too much. I really tried! But finally I pulled off at a rest area and went out back. I don't *think* anybody could see me . . ."

His color heightened yet again. No, but he could hope.

"It's hard to pee no hands, you know, but I had been practicing in the shower. It was such a relief by then . . ." He closed his eyes, the memory of this really big, satisfying piss still sensual for him.

"Was it daylight?"

"Oh, *yes!*"

Steve had gotten to Tahoe and his mistress had done her worst: tied to a rack in a ski cabin, his needy, lonely cock finally handled by her beloved hands, trussed in a complex net of bondage I could not quite imagine even as he explained how she had done it.

"I would think you'd just shoot off, being handled by her after so long without being touched."

Steve glowed. "I would only do it if she made me, or told me to. My cum belonged to her, every drop of it." He looked at me hopefully, but sadly, I could think of no use of my own for Steve's cum.

Then, cock and balls safely encased, she invaded his ass

with a butt plug ("the largest one I've taken so far," he said proudly), then flogged him until he whimpered her name and had to use his safe word.

"What word did she have you use?"

" 'Pink panties,' " he said, smiling.

It came out that Steve was married. He clearly wished to continue to serve me, by which I gathered he meant "eat me out for the rest of the afternoon."

But the phantom wife gave me the opportunity I had been looking for, a reason to abuse him. While not yet savvy about the psyche of the bottom, I felt that as a top I needed to exercise a little discipline.

"Why are you even here?" I demanded. "Why not worship your wife?"

Steve grew uncomfortable. Eyes low, he said, "She's not into it. She doesn't like it."

Fair enough, but as a feminist, I felt I needed to strike at least a small blow on her behalf.

"Then at least I hope you treat her like a queen."

"Oh, Mistress, *you're* my queen . . ."

"Steven! Stop that! I have not given you permission to call me 'Mistress'!" He cowered.

"And if you don't worship women enough to make your wife's life beautiful before you sneak across town hoping to eat pussy, my pussy is not *ever* going to be accessible to you! You selfish man! You are not worthy!"

Still, I passed Steve on to a woman I knew who probably knew what to do with him after he rinsed the soap out of her panties. Even if she only got her kitchen floor cleaned, some good came of it.

I, on the other hand, went to San Francisco to join the people Steve had left behind. I know now that perhaps his wife and he had had a comfortable arrangement . . . though perhaps, like so many submissives, he really *was* a selfish man. It takes time, I suppose, to learn to be selfish—it is a quality some of us could use a little more of.

I think of Steve now and thank him for being the first man to see the goddess in me and to give me the power and deference I am due. Each journey does begin with a single step, and perhaps without him I would never have spanked a butt red or gazed into the eyes of a submissive man—or woman. Perhaps I would never have had the nerve, either, to give myself body and soul to a domina, or to a master.

But only to the very, very worthy. Most of us still blindly chase our worthiness, or do not even know to seek it. Few have found it, but it is well worth the confusing and frightening search. Steve knew this, and now, so do I.

At the Power Exchange

JESSI HOLHART

Beyond the cyclone fence stood a horse, a table, and a cross, each padded and eye-ringed for comfort and creativity. The concrete path outside the fence was lighted by streaks, symbols, and splatters of black-lit paint, and was paced by the lost and hungry herd. Cowboys and sheep men stamped and slinked and strutted around, each hoping for a way in.

Inside the enclosure, bright white spotlights cast criss-crossed lines, leaving dark shadows in the places between. In the spotlight, I danced. The shadows of my hips and arms moved across Janet's shoulders and back. I had already taken off my golden trench coat—it was now draped over a crossbar of the equipment. Writhing rhythmically, I pivoted and twisted my long torso, voluptuous hips, thick thighs, serpentine arms, and long, expressive hands. My four-inch spike-heeled golden thigh-high boots matched my golden satin opera-length gloves and the copper rings and zippers of my attire. Copper zippers ran up the front of each of the legs of my black leather shorts. Copper rings connected at the sides of my black leather vest. Beneath that, a single copper ring in the center of my chest held together the triangles of my top. My long golden hair flashed as I tossed it around in the light, against the flat black back of my vest, across Janet's shoulder where she stood, just one more piece of black equipment in the scene.

Crowds formed against the fence on the two closest sides, reeking with desire.

Janet wore a simple black shirt, black jeans, and black boots. Although just about my size, she had a different build, and carried herself differently. She had light skin and freckles across her face. Her body was tightly packed and muscular, her torso forming a nice "V" between her broad shoulders and her small waist. As dynamic as my motion was, Janet was solid and still to her core. She stood spread-eagled, resting palms on the vertical beams that were positioned for standing bondage. But there were no physical bonds holding her there. She simply stood as I had placed her—face and eyes forward, watching my shadow whenever it fell on the floor or fence in front of her. She could sense me in other ways, too, coming up so close behind her that the air was stirred and softly seasoned by the sweetness of my scent. Then, *zip! ziiip!* And my leather shorts were draped over her shoulder, mixing the smell of leather and passion in her nostrils.

At last I touched her. I leaned against Janet's back and tossed my hair over her shoulder, then turned to drag moist lips up the back of her neck, opening them at the nape to softly bite and growl, sucking teeth, and stepped away. Moments like this always make me salivate. I slapped, punched, and scratched her back and shoulders through her shirt. Janet stood solid as the rain of blows became harder, then softer. I hugged her from behind, clutching her breasts and gyrating against her buttocks before ducking under her arm to stand in front of her. I nuzzled her neck, ran teeth and tongue across her throat. At last I kissed her, taking her lip between my teeth, just to feel it. Finally, I unbuttoned and removed Janet's shirt.

Behind her back again, I pulled a flogger from a small tan bag. I lightly touched her, then licked her back softly with it. I worked up a rhythm that included hard and soft stokes. The long, soft, heavy strips of leather offer a great range of sensations, in the right hands. Alternately I beat her with my hands and fists, just because I like the feel of living skin against mine. After working up a heat, I turned Janet around. When she stared too hard, I slapped her face. Then I took her by the hand and lead her across the space to the horse.

This was a spanking horse. It's similar to a sawhorse in basic construction, with several additions for comfort and convenience. It was taller than your average sawhorse, probably three feet high, and the top was amply padded and roughly eight inches wide, rather than the two inches of a traditional horse. About a foot off the floor, along the side supports of the horse, padded supports had been placed. And this piece of equipment was bolted together very solidly. People of various sizes and shapes could very comfortably kneel on the side supports and rest their body along the wide, padded top.

"Take them off," I instructed, pointing to Janet's pants. After she complied, she was rewarded with a little ride on the horse. While she lay over the horse, I flogged her, gently at first. I was teasing her. She moaned with pleasure when I laid my weight into each stroke. We call this kind of a beating "candy." Then I climbed onto her back, straddling her, and rubbed her ass. I patted her bare, round, tight little butt. I spanked her, rubbing small, hot circles into her cheeks first, then smacked them, rubbed and kissed away the pain, then gave some more. I drummed softly, a syncopated beat, with sharp little surprises imbedded into the musical sounds. Finally, I took out a paddle and, after rubbing her with it, spanked her, hot and hard. As she squirmed under me, I danced and rubbed my wet sex, steaming past the lace tonga across her lower back. We were both panting by the time I dismounted, raised Janet from her knees on the horse, then had her sit on one of the side supports, like a bench.

There were more kisses, and lips guided to kiss . . . breasts, belly, hip, crotch. I took out a long, thick, smooth white length of rope. Taking Janet's thumbs into my hand, I stretched her arm out straight onto her knees. Then, I took the simple loop of the middle of the doubled-over rope. Feeding the ends through this loop, I began wrapping her up from the wrists. I wrapped firmly, but not tightly, up her arms to her shoulders, securing it there with a simple knot. Loops of rope wrapped around her arms. Then I repeated the action around her neck, making lovely even bands of white like a stack of African neck rings, white as pearls. I made these loops loose enough that I could hook my fingers between her throat and each strand of the rope. I held her as if by a shirt collar and, tugging, dragged her from the bench, and then back again.

Glancing over her shoulder, I caught sight of the sea of eyes, hunched and huddled and pressing against the fence. There were too many, too close, mere inches from us, on the other side of the fence. My eyes narrowed, feeling protective and fierce. Both of my fists clenched. I looked at Janet, lovely, strong, and vulnerable, and my lip curled into a snarl. I reached into the bag beside us and pulled out an African club. Our audience caught their breath. The club is a carved piece of wood, about a foot and a half long, with a thick knob at one end. I swung it wide, hitting the fence with such force that the length of it moved back nearly a foot and the crowd backed up with it. One witness, too close and not quick enough, held his nose. I smiled wickedly, catching the look of embarrassment on his face. Then I turned back to my prize, limp in my grasp, eyes closed. I slapped hard, then slapped again. At last she opened her eyes to me. She was completely accepting, completely open to me. That made me smile. And it made me wet. I set her firmly onto the bench again, and knelt in front of her to release the ropes around her arms first. I unwrapped her arms, revealing the soft, symmetrical pattern of indentations the rope left on them. Lovely. I climbed the horse, to sit on the highest part, and turned Janet around to face me there. I used her rope collar one last time, to guide her face to my thighs.

"Kiss," I said, and she did. At my command, her kisses made a path up my thighs to my crotch. Carefully, I pulled the loops from her neck, one loop at a time, until she was free. Then I motioned to the bag. "Get a glove," I told her. She went to the bag and reached into it. She raised her head with an inquiring look and held up a bottle of lube with the glove. I nodded, biting my lips impatiently. Stretching a bit, I took a few deep breaths and looked again at those who had been watching. I did not recognize a single face, but they knew me well enough that eyes averted at my solid gaze. Janet stood ready, awaiting my next move. I stood, moving softly to the music, and then danced a few steps. I leaned against one of the pillars in the center of the enclosure. I took the gloves and lube and motioned Janet to my feet.

"Kiss," I directed. "Twenty." She stretched herself out at my feet, arms spread to shoulder width, and groaned. She did twenty push-ups, kissing my feet passionately at the bottom of each one. The last two are always my favorites, when her muscles strain and she shakes with the effort. Then she knelt at my feet and looked up. I pressed my panties to her face, rubbing myself with her nose. I handed her the glove and lube. "Put it on," I said. Then I had her fist me while I masturbated. I spun on her hand, turning so I could bend over and lean my face against the cool steel of the pillar. When we were done, Janet wrapped me in the robe she pulled like magic from the bag, the last of our tricks to come out. I sat, as Janet cleaned up.

She escorted me out, and the crowds stepped back to make way. When we sat, giving ourselves a moment to unwind, a man offered his services, and thanked us when we allowed him to bring us something to eat and drink. I think I knew the watchers, when we brushed past them. They seemed to thank us with their eyes, staying back enough to give us room and peace. I thanked them, too, in my heart. An audience can be a very hot thing.

Submission—
The Softer Side of S&M

LILYCAT

o, the safe word will be platypus," he says as they leave. The bartender, cleaning the bar nearby, lets out a half laugh. The bartender has been holding back the laughter since the exiting couple had met and started downing Roy Rogers.

They started talking when she, with her cute "Hello Kitty" T-shirt cut at the neckline and her bright red hair, leaned across the bar to ask for a Band-Aid for the drunken man, who had stumbled out of the mosh pit with a gash on his head. The man wasn't as interested in getting treatment as he was in rejoining the mosh, so he left before the bandage could be applied.

"I guess he doesn't want help. He'd rather just bleed," the

man at the bar said, looking up from his journal. His light, steel blue eyes peered out from behind his glasses. He sported a typical concertgoer uniform—band T-shirt, faded jeans, and Doc Martens. He could have been mistaken for just another concertgoer except he had been sitting at the bar for an hour, writing.

"No, I guess he doesn't want help," she replied as her eyes met his, then she quickly and shyly looked down at her boots. "Isn't it hard to write here?"

"No, I always listen to this type of music when I write at home," he said, then leaned in toward her. "And I'm sort of getting off on the energy of the crowd. It's inspiring." He patted the bar stool next to him, which had just become empty. She sat down.

They talked about favorite bands and authors, and told their life stories over the music coming from the stage. The conversation gradually moved toward the erotic: kinky and strange sexual activities they have done.

"I don't really understand S&M," she said, sipping her fourth Roy Rogers. "Pain just hurts me."

"S&M is about more than just giving and receiving physical pain," he said, adjusting his glasses. "It's about power. It's about giving and getting control. It is about domination and submission."

"I guess I understand submission and control. I have times in relationships—sexual . . ." she said as she cleared her throat, "when I want to be in control of the whole situation. And other times I'm in the mood for someone else to be in control, and to just be taken."

"Which mood are you in tonight?" he inquired, and she began to blush.

"Umm . . . I don't know," she said with a giggle.

"Want to play a game?"

"What sort of game?"

"I want to show you the softer side of S&M—submission and seduction," he answered.

"It sounds like a commercial for perfume, but I'm game. What do you have in mind?"

"I'd like to take you to my house, and see what I can do to make you beg to be taken," he says, as he gets off his stool and puts his hand out for her to take.

She does.

A short cab ride later, they arrive at his studio apartment, where it is a few quick steps to the bed. They tumble onto it in a silly, giggling embrace.

All during the cab ride, they joked about scenes in movies and lines in songs that get them hot. They ran fingertips across each other's various body parts, and planted quick kisses on each other's necks in between laughs.

He breaks away from the lip lock they had begun, and says, "We should start the game now."

"You're serious about getting me to beg to have you?" she replies.

"Yes." He reaches for a basket under the bed and pulls out a pair of handcuffs.

"What are you going to do with those?" she asks, a slight quiver in her voice.

He looks her straight in the eyes and gently lays her on the

26

bed, takes her hands above her head and handcuffs them together. He pulls her shirt up and undoes her bra.

She begins to squirm, as he laps his tongue quickly at her nipples and breathes warmly up and down her breasts. He lightly bites her left nipple and she bucks in reply.

"Slow down, horsie, we don't want you saying 'platypus' too soon here. I want to have some fun teasing you first."

"Don't worry about me saying 'platypus,' 'cause *you* are going to be the one submitting first and saying that word," she says as she suddenly wraps her legs tightly around his waist, softly grabs hold of his bottom lip with her lips, and pulls him into a kiss.

He breaks away from the kiss and says, "Hey, frisky, you aren't supposed to top from the bottom."

"Why not? Maybe we should make this game a contest and see who says 'platypus' first." She giggles.

"What does the winner get?"

"Sex in a position she, or I guess maybe he, wants."

"Will I get to have you in only one of my favorite positions when I win?" he asks as he returns to kissing her.

"When *I* win . . ." she says, and she lines her damp crotch up to the hard cock bulging through his jeans and begins to slowly grind into him. "I have a few positions *I* like . . ." She begins to bite his neck. "Doggie style with you grabbing hold of my ass as you mount me, or running your fingers down my back as you thrust into me." She bit his chest through his shirt. "Or sixty-nine with your cock completely in my mouth, and as I suck, you fuck me with your tongue and lick up all my wetness," she continues as she runs her tongue up his neck. "Or maybe we could do it missionary style, so we could stay in this position. I could even stay handcuffed. We would just need to get our pants off. Oh, and you'll need to say 'platypus.'"

He stares into her eyes as she begins to work her jeaned pussy even harder into his penis. Neither one wants to be the first to break eye contact. She grinds into him relentlessly. It doesn't take much longer before he moans, "Platypus."

Tagging Along

JANE CASSELL

he rule is this. Don't embarrass me in front of my friends, and by this I mean walk behind us and don't talk unless I talk to you first, or let you know that it's okay. If you think you can possibly do this, I'll let you tag along!"

I had just started dating a younger man. He was a hot twenty-eight-year-old bi babe who'd graduated with a degree in literature from Wintergreen, a fancy West Coast liberal arts college. We'd met at some smoky, pretentious, excessively hip art party and I'd brought him home. He was funny, smart, cute, and sweet with doe eyes and pouty lips. I don't usually go for younger, pretty boys, but he was persistent, and sometimes persistence wins out.

After the second date I told him that there were several

things he needed to agree to if he wanted to continue to see me, including that our relationship was to remain open to other people, that SM be a part of our sexual play, and that he understand that my need for privacy was extremely important in my day-to-day life. He eagerly agreed to participate and respect all my stipulations, but then told me that he was an SM virgin. He confided that he'd enjoyed reading the Marquis de Sade and thought he might like SM, but thought leather and role-playing hokey. On the other hand, I'd enjoyed leather and role-playing, but thought the Marquis de Sade was hokey, so I supposed we were even. However, he said he was "open" to leather and role-playing. I wasn't quite sure what being "open" meant, but went along with it. I was pretty sure he'd hang himself with it and I'd get what I wanted.

This is how we found ourselves two weeks later getting ready to go on Cedar City's monthly art opening marathon. The idea was that we would go from gallery to gallery, I'd network with the art boys and diss all their seminal work behind their backs, and Sean would tag along. By then I had found out that Sean was a lot of fun to be around, so the thought of exploring the play possibilities with him was beginning to sound very appealing.

I decided we'd start with a little role-playing for my role-playing-phobic bad boy. I would be the older juvenile delinquent schoolgirl and he would be the whiny younger brother who wanted to tag along. That's when I said: "The rule is this. Don't embarrass me in front of my friends, and by this I mean walk behind us and don't talk unless I talk to you first, or let you know that it's okay. If you think you can possibly do this, I'll let you tag along!"

I gave Sean a pair of blue jeans, a blue-and-green-striped T-shirt, and high-tops to wear, and then laid out my clothes. He was charmingly nervous with excitement over his first real SM experience, so I thought it was time to give him something to be nervous about. I put on my white oxford shirt, brushed some imaginary lint off my shirt, then tore it off and threw it on the floor.

"Damn it! If I'm going to let you go out with me, then the least you can do is have my shirt prepared when I need to get dressed! Why isn't this ironed? Iron it right now and use starch. I want sharp sleeve creases, and pay special attention to the collar. I hate a messy collar."

Sean gaped. It was one thing to read about eighteenth-century French royalty pissing on peasant girls, it's quite another thing to have the gal you've been happily fucking for the past three weeks start bossing you around. I grabbed him by his arm, drew him close, asked him if he was stupid or deaf, and repeated my request. As he scurried to pick up my shirt, I was happy to see that he looked even cuter when stunned.

I swore at him as I buttoned up my shirt, knotted my tie, and pulled up my plaid Catholic schoolgirl skirt. I put on white cotton panties, white knee socks, and oxfords, then threw my leather jacket over the perverse train wreck that I called fetish wear. "Don't make me regret that I brought you with me! If you talk to my friends or get in the way, you'll be sorry!"

We left the apartment with Sean looking curiously chastened and a little worried. I felt a bit edgy with first-time nerves, but eager to put him through his paces, take him home, beat him, then fuck him. But he didn't know about all that.

Once we reached the gentrified art district, we parked, got out, and started walking toward the first art gallery. At first Sean fell in step by my side, until I snarled, "Look kid, who do you think you are? I told you that I'm just letting you come along as a favor. If you get anywhere near me, I'll send you packing! Now walk behind me and behave!"

The first show was a collection of fetish photos by someone I knew locally. He was fond of posing his models looking moody and wearing a lot of expensive shiny black corset-y stuff with laces, zippers, and buckles. They all had dark red lipstick, retro hairstyles, and remote distracted looks, like they were trying to remember if they needed to pick up some kitty litter and coffee on the way home from the photo shoot. He'd shot them in kitschy motel interiors with overturned lamps and the vague impression of catastrophe and claustrophobia.

When we got to the gallery, the photographer was standing near the wine table with several of his models cooing and hanging about him. I toured the room, decided his work was getting icier by the year, then went over to congratulate him on "yet another fine show of wonderfully erotic pieces," and introduce him to my "young friend." Sean remembered his age for the night, and mumbled a shy "hello," shuffled his feet, and tried not to look at the models' breasts. The photographer raised one carefully groomed black eyebrow at the words "young friend" and my odd outfit, then looked Sean up and down. I was very pleased. I felt very naughty displaying Sean to my colleague, and knew word would soon be out that I was up to no good. Artists do like their gossip. I smiled, told Sean to come along, and we left for the next gallery.

The next show, a group show of academic still life and landscape paintings, was a few blocks away, but the night was beautiful and I was in no hurry to get there. I was enjoying having such a contrite little boy following me, but needed to be careful not to let him know this. I could hear him dragging his sneakers, so I admonished him and told him he'd be punished for that later. I also told him I'd caught him ogling the models' nipples at the previous gallery, that he was way too young for such shenanigans, and that this was yet another infraction. He seemed surprised at how quickly his mistakes were adding up and bit his lip with worry. I could see chapters from the Marquis de Sade's *The 120 Days of Sodom* flitting through his head as he tried to imagine what I could possibly do to him once we were home. I stifled a giggle as I remembered how anxious I was the first time I'd ever been beaten. I remembered how I'd both looked forward to it but was also afraid I'd be disappointed or displease my lover. I loved imagining these same thoughts in Sean's mind as he walked behind me.

At Axis Collective, the next gallery, we ran into another of my art cohorts. Karen was a performance and video artist whose work was genuinely cutting-edge and interesting. I was always pleased to see her, but she knew Sean and this could become tricky. Well, trickier—and in a very good way. Karen had been in an SM relationship for the past fifteen years, and I'd already told her that I wanted to play with Sean sometime soon. It was an unexpected pleasure to have her show up to boss around my new boyfriend.

I grinned and said, "Sean is my kid brother tonight. I'm letting him tag along, but he hasn't been behaving very well. He's tried to walk near me, drags his heels, and has been staring at strange girls' breasts. He's been totally fucking obnoxious!"

Karen caught on right away, made a harrumph noise, and frowned at Sean. She turned to me and suggested that we stroll down to the Hi-Lo Diner for something to eat. We left the gallery and Karen and I meandered arm and arm to the restaurant, occasionally yelling back for Sean to stop dawdling.

After we got to the Hi-Lo and got a table, Karen put on her glasses, peered at Sean as severely as a short, middle-aged performance artist could, and asked why he had been such a terribly bad, bad boy. I could tell Sean couldn't decide if he should laugh, but I really wanted the evening to end with his cute butt hot and pink, and my pussy around his dick, so I nudged him, hissed sinisterly, "Tell her why you've been so bad," then winked at him. I could see him becoming more resolved to continue our game as he hung his head. He then blushingly confessed that he really wanted to be with us and hang out with us because we were the cool older girls. Karen patted his hand tenderly and told him he was very sweet, but that he needed to work on being respectful and good around his older sister. She reminded him that older sisters always know what is best for their brothers.

I could tell Karen was getting a kick out of our dalliance as we all finished our food. I was so turned on by Sean and our game that I could hardly eat. Sean squirmed as he picked at his sandwich. Finally Karen decided to drive home, leaving us to continue our fun.

I drove us to Sean's apartment on the north side of town in my old battle-scarred silver VW Beetle. He lived by himself in a neatly kept blue-collar neighborhood. I hadn't visited his place before and was pleasantly surprised at its hominess. He lived in one side of an older half double that he'd bought and renovated. As we started up the front walkway, he explained that he had inherited his dad's plumbing business after he had graduated from college and had done well for himself fixing pipes. I sneered and growled that I had a couple of pipes he could help clear . . . if he felt up to it. He batted his long lashes, cast his eyes to the sidewalk modestly, and whispered that he'd be honored if I'd allow him to be "up to it" later that night.

There were several bushes flanking the wooden steps leading to Sean's front porch. I stopped Sean and ordered him to cut himself a couple of thin branches from the bushes. He hesitated, but did as I told him. My pussy had been getting progressively wetter throughout the evening, and the sight of Sean kneeling at my feet gathering switches made me even damper. Once inside, I pushed Sean against the dark foyer wall and instructed him to remove all of his clothing and take me to his bedroom.

Once upstairs, I looked around the room. He slept on a narrow, prim bed covered with a wool log cabin quilt. His room was full of books, both on shelves and stacked in piles along the edges of the bedroom. The room was lit by a dim, stained-glass reading lamp on a small, high, antique bedside table. A bottle of lube and a down-turned copy of *The Leather Daddy and the Femme* were on the bedside table. I was glad to see that he'd finally made it to this century. There wasn't much in the room besides the bed, table, books, a naked man, and me. It seemed like a winning combination.

I ordered him to take his pocketknife and peel the bark from the two pieces of wood he'd taken from the bushes. Sean sat on his bed peeling the switches. His hands were trembling and his dick was hard. It made me even more excited to see that he was as turned on as I was, and I wanted to let him know this. I unloosened my tie, unbuttoned the top few buttons of my shirt, and rubbed my nipples through my white lace bra. "Baby, you make me so hot when you do what I tell you to do. I love watching you hold that knife naked, with your dick poking up. You'd better not cut it, because I have plans for your dick."

Sean blushed and his dick's head glistened with precum. With one final long stroke he finished peeling the stick, stood up, and held the two switches out to me. I felt both totally thrilled and completely gleeful as I took a switch in one hand and caressed his bare butt with the other. He had a lovely hard, round ass, with two lower back dimples accenting its swell. My hard nipples touched his chest lightly as we stood facing each other. I reached for his face, holding him by his jaw, brought him close to me, and kissed him. It was the first kiss we'd exchanged that evening, and for a minute I relaxed into the kiss's warmth and sexiness. I let the kiss continue, gently grabbing and pulling the hair near the nape of his neck, softly stroking his ass and back, while becoming more and more turned on. I slapped his ass a few times to remind him of the possibilities, letting my blows become progressively harder as our kiss became progressively deeper. I cupped his ass, reaching around to caress his balls.

When I was certain that Sean had forgotten about the switch, I quickly stopped our kiss and turned him around. Surprise is always important. I sat on the side of the monkish bed and commanded him to lie over my lap. He looked both turned on and nervous. I started stroking his ass lightly, so he could get used to the different feel of the switch. I wasn't sure how hard he could take it and wanted to stop before it slid away from sensual pain to "Hey, that really hurts!" pain. He had told me he had been turned on by the Marquis de Sade, but reading about pain and experiencing it on your bare skin is something else entirely. I wanted him to want to do this with me again, so I felt I needed to take it slow for his first time.

I wiggled a little, the heaviness of Sean thrown over my lap intensifying the sensation that traveled from my ass, up my pussy, to my clit. I felt his hard-on through my skirt and the thought of it inside my wet pussy made me shiver. I slid my fingers under his belly and to his stiff, smooth dick, giving it a rub and tug to remind him of later possibilities, then I slapped his gorgeous ass with my other hand. I hit him five times with my palm, removed my other hand from his dick, and stroked his back from the nape of his neck on down to his adorable butt dimples. Reaching beside me, I grabbed the switch and hit him three times, with each blow a little harder than the previous one. Sean gasped and gave a tiny whimper.

"It's a good thing you prepared this stick. You must have realized what a little monster you were tonight while we were out. I don't know if I'll let you tag along again after that episode!" At this, I hit him two additional times with the switch he'd prepared so diligently, and started to stand up.

"I'm sorry," he whimpered sweetly. "I tried to be good. Please don't go!"

I settled myself down on the bed again. "Here are the problems. First of all, you were dawdling; second, you dragged your heels; third, you looked lustfully at older women's breasts; fourth, you talked to Karen without my permission;

and fifth, you left imperfections on this switch when you stripped it!"

"I'm so sorry. I promise to behave next time. Please don't leave. I'll do anything."

"Well," and I hit him once with some force, "if you are very, very contrite and well mannered tonight, I might think about bringing you along again. But I need to see some real cooperation, none of this squealing and wiggling. How do I know you won't be a whining, sniveling, obnoxious little brat again the next time we go out?" I caressed his butt with the switch and gave it a light tap.

"What can I do? How can I prove to you that I'll be good?"

"You'll need to be punished for your disrespectful and disobedient behavior. We'll have to wait and see what comes after that!" I was hoping that what would be coming afterward was me, then Sean in quick succession, but didn't let on to Sean. I wanted to keep him wondering.

I settled in to beat Sean until his butt was warm and glowing pink. Holding his broad, muscular shoulders firmly with my right hand, I started hitting him with the switch in my left hand. After an initial sharp intake of breath, Sean's breathing was even. I could tell that my actions were having the desired effect by the wetness leaking from his dickhead and the litany of apologies falling from his lips. Between the heat and pressure of his body pressed against my groin, and the delight of hitting him, I started to orgasm. I threw the switch to the floor and held Sean's reddened ass in my hand as my pussy tightened and spasmed.

Once I finished coming and gotten my bearings, I quickly turned Sean over, raised him up, sat on his lap, and kissed him for the second time that night. His lips were soft, then hard. His hands pushed my skirt up to my waist, and drew my panties aside. With a grunt, he roughly shoved his dick inside my hot pussy. I wanted him inside me now. I wanted to feel his dick buried inside my pussy as deeply as possible, and he gave me exactly what I wanted. I grabbed my nipples and twisted them as he held my ass. I felt his finger press up against my asshole. He started pressing my asshole in a circular motion.

"Oh, little brother, fuck me hard . . . do it . . ." And with several long moans, I came for the second time that night. Hearing my orgasm, Sean started the series of groans that signaled the start of his orgasm and thrust with greater vigor. It felt like he was fucking me all the way up to my throat. He came with a roar and a yell.

Breathing heavily, we held each other and started laughing. I licked his neck, then found his lips with mine. Our kiss tasted salty from sex and sweat, and I knew this was only the first fuck of the night.

Afters

M. CHRISTIAN

*M*r. Blue called just as I was putting away the last of the toys. Don't know why I answered it. Still, clients like Blue keep the dollars coming in, and as we had this fuckin' great phone bill stuck to the fridge with a fancy magnet, I like to think that it was my wallet and not, well, for any other reason that I picked up the damn phone.

He had masturbated. It took a couple of rote "I asked you not to call me after hours, slave," "How dare you interrupt your mistress, worm," and even a "Do you want me to be displeased?" before he finally spilled it (ha ha) and I remembered: He wasn't supposed to wank till our next session on Wednesday. I was tired, so I really didn't put that much work into my solution: "Stick a candle up your ass for twenty minutes, and don't you dare touch your dick till I tell you to!"

I didn't wait for an answer—just clicked it off during his "Yes, Mistress" ramble. Deep breath, deep breath—it wasn't that dealing with clients like Blue was tough, it was just that it had been a very, very long week, and the one thing that had kept me going through the endless whippings, the countless clothespins, and the god-knows-how-many "Now you can jerk off, slave" routines was the thought of hanging up my toys and getting out that door.

Then the phone rang. Two things ran through my mind as I hung up my prized Jay Marsten flogger: one was Nina looking at me smugly as I tried to explain why I was late, and the other was having to scrape together enough coins to pay my bills.

In the end, dollars won and, with a theatrical sigh, I picked up the phone. Mr. Red was having a fashion crisis. For the manager of a high-end realty company with a wife, three kids, and a ridiculous mortgage, he certainly sounded like a tweaking queen. It took a little work, more of the old routine, before I got him to breathe deeply and tell me what the problem was. When he told me, I tried, real hard, not to laugh into the receiver—it doesn't help the image of Mistress Divine, Slave Master Extraordinare, to laugh at her clients . . . at least not with a high-pitch squeal of childish delight.

In the end I told Red to calm down ("slut") and to just ("you silly girl") use panty hose instead of his torn fishnets ("and don't bother mommy at work again"), and then, gratefully, hung up.

The dungeon was quiet. It was nice, but something nicer was waiting for me back at our little apartment. I checked my watch and gasped: I was due home in a little over half an hour. Damn, Nina would be real pissed if I was late. I took a quick scan of the room, checking out the stocks, the massage table, the sling, the toy box, and all the rest—trying to see what I had to put away and what could stay out till Saturday and my next client. Unfortunately, I still had to wipe the table, the sling, and the braces of the cross down with hydrogen peroxide—a fifteen-minute job, at least.

I was ten minutes into it when the phone rang again. No domestic money worries this time, I thought of Nina—scowling and pacing back and forth—and picked it right up.

Mr. Yellow this time. I swallowed a reflexive *shit* and snapped him a sharp "How dare you call your mistress? Didn't I say that you were never to call her after six o'clock . . . ?" and so forth, trying to get a quick, humble apology and a hang up.

No dice. Mr. Yellow needed help. Running the mantra of *pays the bills, pays the bills, pays the bills*, I dropped the hostility and switched to bored concern: "What is it *this* time, slave?"

At least Yellow was a lot more forthcoming. His Prince Albert was really inflamed and sore, it seemed. Calmly, dropping Mistress Divine enough to show concern, but not too much—after all, he had to listen to me—I told him to clean it carefully and put some Neosporin on it, and call me in another day or so with a report on how it was doing.

That was it, right there: Mistress Divine was "Closed," she had spun the sign around, put out the cat (metaphorically), and locked the door behind her.

She was going home to a very well deserved, and much needed, relaxing evening with her precious Nina.

I was lucky, damned lucky, that she was in a good mood when I walked in the door, even understanding. "Hard day at the office?" she said, handing me a cold drink after I'd shucked my coat.

I tried not to smile, tried to keep my face still as I accepted the glass and sipped it. After a nice swallow I handed it back and slowly got down on my knees before her: "Yes, Mistress; sorry I'm late, Mistress."

"I understand, slut, but that doesn't mean you escape punishment."

"Yes, Mistress," I said, feeling smaller, more fragile, younger—but more and more precious by the moment. "I understand."

"Good, I'm glad you do," she said with a delightful touch of sarcasm, walking up to me and putting a hand under my chin. Lifting my head, she looked into my eyes, searching my irises. "Now take off your clothes and meet me in the bedroom."

My world was usually black leather, rubber, latex, and, sometimes, surgical steel. It was full of cowering men, boot kissing, and endless days of hearing "Yes, Mistress." I enjoyed it, and it was something I was good at, but it wasn't me.

At the doorway, I kicked off my shoes, pulled off my sweatshirt, unsnapped my bra, shucked my pants, and threw my panties in a far corner. Our place was small, but not tiny; it had light, charm, and a surprisingly big bedroom. It had to have that, because our brass bed wasn't small.

That bed was our world, our oasis, our temple, our sanctuary. Looking at it, I was filled with a warm glow, a sense of having arrived. I was home . . . home with my mistress.

I felt her hand on the square of my back, a gentle touch. "You are my precious, but you were also late—and you know how much I dislike you being late."

The venom in her words was a sour-candy performance, but as always it touched me very deep down. I wasn't going to be punished: I was wanted, desired, loved.

"Yes, Mistress," I said as I turned and bowed my head. "I understand."

"You know what to do. Get ready."

I went to the bed, climbed onto its thick cloud of comforters. I stretched out, facedown in the mountain of pillows, and spread my legs just a bit.

"You are mine, slut. You know that—you belong to me. You are mine to play with, to use for my pleasure, and to hurt if I need to. But you also know that I'm here with you, that I will always treat my favorite toy very well."

"Yes, Mistress," I said, turning my head slightly. "I understand."

"So, slut, how many minutes were you late?"

I hadn't noticed it in my rush to get home. My mind raced—I guessed: "Fifteen minutes, Mistress."

"Wrong, slut—" Nina said, kneeling beside me on the bed, "it was twenty. So, for you, twenty-five: twenty for each minute you were late, and five for not keeping track."

"Yes, Mistress," I said, already feeling my body start to respond to the ritual, the performance, to being home with Nina, my owner.

"I think the flogger tonight," she said, getting up and moving to the toy chest—our personal toy chest. Turning my head to bury my face in the comforters, I heard the hinges squeak, heard the tumble of leather, and then the lid slowly shutting.

"Twenty-five . . ." the first was light, a warm-up. The heavy strands of the leather flogger falling almost gently across my ass. Their touch was electric, almost shocking—and I felt a body thrill race up my spine. The next touch was harder, more focused, and I felt the muscles of my ass tense just afterward—anticipating the next and harder blow.

One after another, each stroke of the whip gaining in intensity, power, force . . . to call it pain would be a half-truth. Nina was good, very good, and the escalation of her whipping was carefully orchestrated. It was a massage at first, the strands beating down on my ass with a glorious tempo, but then it became deeper, harder, and I started to . . . drift. Part of my mind was there, on that great bed, having my ass whipped, but another part of me was floating high above, entranced by the bodily sensations she was driving through me.

Harder, harder, harder—my back arched, my ass tensed, my hands clawed at the bedspreads. My breathing grew faster, faster, faster, as each stroke landed heavier. There was pain, but there was also ecstasy—and both of them were good.

Then it was done. My ass throbbed rhythmically, matching my hammering heartbeat. My breath was ragged—each intake, each exhale, charged with a quavering excitement—and I was aware, distantly, that my cunt was very, very wet.

"Good, slut, very good. You took your punishment well, very well indeed. I would almost think you enjoyed it."

"Yes, Mistress," I said, panting heavily.

"Ah, but then you are a slut, aren't you? So, of course you enjoyed it, didn't you?"

"Yes, Mistress, I enjoyed it. I enjoyed it very much."

"So show me, slut. Show me how much you enjoyed it."

Yes . . . yes, I wanted to show her. Very much I wanted to show her. Slowly, I rolled over, gasping as my ass rubbed gently across the stitched comforter, until I could see her. Nina stood beside the bed, still in her jeans and T-shirt, small, hard tits visible through the thin materials, nipples twin dark points that instantly made my mouth water.

"Show me, slut. Show your mistress."

I spread my legs, cautiously, feeling the muscles in my ass strain against the movement, until they were wide open. Then I put my fingers down to my cunt lips and pulled them apart, feeling my wetness in all its throbbing glory. "See, Mistress?"

"Yes, slut, I do see. I see your very red, very wet lips; I see your clit, so big and hard, twitching with a hunger for my tongue, my touch. I see you—I see my slut."

I was flowing, and could feel my clit pulsing deep and primordially down among the folds of my labia.

"I know what you want, slut. I know you too well. I know you want my lips down there between your hard thighs, you want my tongue to flicker across that hard little bead. But that's not going to happen, slut. No, not at all. Instead, I want you to show me, demonstrate for your mistress, just how big a slut you are. Show me, girl; put a hand down there and feel yourself, touch that beating bead in your cunt. Come for me, slut; come for me good and hard."

I did. With her eyes smiling at me, I put my right hand down between my sweat-slick thighs and touched, at first, the hard point of my clit. That first contact was as shocking as the initial touch of her whip, as if a spark had jumped from my quivering finger to the pinpoint of my burning desire.

Then I really did: tapping, circling, stroking, I fell into my regular rhythm, my self-performance of jerking off. The actions may have been familiar, but the heat was tremendous, blistering—not just because of the whip, not just because of the words, Nina's performance, but because she was watching me: My wonderful mistress was watching my fingers dance and stir my molten cunt.

For her, because of her, I came—a body eruption, a wild explosion of quivering muscles. Against my will, my eyes closed, my legs closed suddenly around my hand, and my throat opened and I called—a deep, throaty bellow of release and joy.

"Such a good slut," my mistress said, stripping and climbing into the bed next to me, mixing her glowing heat with mine. "Such a wonderful, wonderful slut."

Before slipping into a good sleep, I pulled myself next to her, content, happy, and glowing: I was a very good slut; and for my mistress, I was the best slut in the whole world.

Paul in the Hospital

CLÉO DUBOIS AND MARGO LIN

*D*ear Madame,

I am writing to thank you for all that I learned from you about being submissive while exploring my fantasies in your dungeon. It helped me through a difficult time in my life. Three months ago I had a serious heart attack, which came as a big surprise since I have none of the usual risk factors. Luckily, I got prompt and expert medical attention and, after a week in the hospital, I began to work on rehabilitation. I went back to work and am doing pretty well.

My training with you as a submissive really helped me through the experience. How? First of all, it helped me deal with pain, how to assess it and cope with it. When asked how much I hurt, I could tell them with some accuracy because I had a benchmark for pain: the white-light pain of nipple clamps coming off after a long time on.

One time you tightened a clamp onto my nipple, ever so slowly, all the while asking me to rate the pain I was experiencing on a scale from one to ten, with ten being the most pain I could take. As my nipple was squeezed harder and harder, the sensation grew more intense, redder, hotter. I wanted to please you so I kept minimizing the ratings. I could see you enjoyed my suffering and I wanted to give you more and more. After the clamps were on, I knew I could sink into the pain, maybe forget it for a moment or two. I could adjust to the pain for the pleasure that it gave you. At times, it even felt warm and comforting having the clamps holding me so tightly.

When you removed the first clamp, after the seemingly endless stream of other tortures, intense white blindness flooded my body. Comfort came from my agonized scream. It took time to catch my breath. Another one-to-ten rating scale came to mind, an order of magnitude larger than the previous one. Then I realized there was another clamp yet to be removed. I had a one hundred level of pain coming when the next nipple clamp was removed. This memory helped me assess levels of pain during the medical procedures that were to come in the ensuing months.

In your dungeon, pain turns me on, but at the clinic it does not. In your presence and within the sensual reality of your chamber, I need the pain, I want the pain, I crave the pain. But pain in a true medical context is different from pain inflicted by your mistress, whom you trust, with whom you negotiate your terms. Our sessions helped me better cope with the pain from the needles and catheters used by medical personnel. I used the slow deep breathing, relaxing into the sensation rather than fighting it, which I learned from you.

I have signed a contract with you to submit to "therapy, treatment, training, and instruction involving sensory enhancements, deprivations, pain applications, and localized application of various devices." I yearn to abide by it. I long for you to experiment on me. It is fun to fantasize, contemplate, desire being used by you in a variety of ways.

I remember being subject to your complete control. The memory kept me company as a nurse started to insert a catheter. I imagined her saying your words, "You have no option but to accept my patient preparation. No complaints. Just relax and surrender. This is but a taste of what is to come!" I began to sink into my private world of sensation as you taught me. I crave it so much.

For a short time after my heart attack, I had to use a mask to sleep at night. It was hard, but your expert gag training and insistence that I practice sucking cock (using those dildos) helped me relax my throat and accept the slightly smothering, invasive masks. The ass fuckings you gave me with dildos made it easier to deal with doctors examining my prostate. I learned how to relax and accept intrusion.

Equal in importance to training in pain endurance has been my training as a submissive. I have been more open to what doctors and nurses have to teach me, more open to listening and learning, and following their orders and instructions. This is hard for adults to do. In the rest of my life I instruct others. I usually don't like to be told what to do. You helped me get into a trusting space with skilled people who want to take me somewhere else (in this case to better health). I learned from you how to surrender my body and to trust them with it.

Of course, they want me to diet, exercise, and reduce stress. This requires discipline. It reminds me of the discipline of corset training, learning to walk in three-inch heels, your instruction in the proper curtsey for a cross-dressed sissy maid. I remember the importance of discipline when I'm at the gym, at dinner, at the scale checking my weight.

Nurse Gladys, my rehab nurse, would make a great dominant. I had thought I would sit quietly on my couch for, say, the next ten years. But she would have none of that. She got me on exercise machines, made me pump iron. She exhorted me to change my diet and reduce the stress in my life, using flip charts to prove her points while I was "chained" to the treadmill. She could have had a whip in her hand. She said most people want to do what they have always done—eat fatty foods and sit around watching television—but still get healthier. They're not open to instruction and to the discipline it requires. I've tried to do as she demanded. Yes, Mistress. Thank you, Mistress. Please, Mistress.

Do you know that I have visited you monthly for fifteen years now? Our rituals of pain, humiliation, and submission mean so much to me. These memories have brought me such pleasure, and continue to do so. Years ago, when I contacted you about fulfilling my fantasies, I did not know that some of them would come close to the truth of my later experiences. It made those experiences less terrifying. Even during the worst of it, it amused me sometimes to think about our sessions while I was in hospitals and doctors' offices. If they only knew what I was thinking about as they poked and prodded.

Now I realize that I won't be able to see you as often as I have in the past due to my health concerns. We won't be able to share some of our favorites activities, such as electrical play. Though this makes me sad, I know we still have many good experiments ahead of us. I want to thank you for the help you gave me during the medical procedures I had to endure. Thank you, Madame.

Yours, in devoted submission,
Paul

The Rubber Chicken Scene

GRETA CHRISTINA

First of all," I told Annabelle, "I do not want you to address me as Sir or Ma'am. Those terms are not sufficiently respectful. I want you to address me as The Great and Powerful Oz."

Annabelle snickered. I smacked her lightly on the ass and turned to Austin. "And yourself, my dear?"

"Oh, The Big Enchilada, for the moment," she replied airily. "But that's *Mr.* Big Enchilada to you, young lady," she told Annabelle. "Don't you be putting on airs with me."

Austin, with her incomparable fashion sense that combined the best of the nineteenth-century English dandy and the San Francisco butch dyke, had once again risen to the occasion, with a black leather vest, knee-high motorcycle boots, a bur-

gundy smoking jacket with a silly-looking gold dragon em-
broidered on the back, and a black bowler hat with a small
British flag tucked into the band. I, on the other hand, had
opted for basic femmey black, a deceptively simple outfit I'd
put together after an hour and a half of tossing my entire
wardrobe around my room shrieking, "I don't have a thing to
wear!"

Annabelle was naked. Per our instructions, she had
stripped down before we arrived, and was now wearing nothing
but gym socks and combat boots. The Bastille was a lovely
dungeon, but its floors left something to be desired. Austin
and I may have been sadists, but we weren't monsters.

I picked up my toy bag and waggled it at Annabelle. Now,
normally, my toy bag contains rather dull, unimaginative devices: whips, paddles, handcuffs, dildos, latex gloves, nipple
clamps, and other such timeworn classics. This evening, however, was different.

This evening, the toy bag contained: a pair of Groucho
glasses, complete with nose and mustache; an arrow-through-
the-head; a lime-green Afro wig eighteen inches in diameter; a
tape of Leonard Nimoy reading bad poetry to the accompani-
ment of light classical music; a Sony Walkman; a seven-foot
beach towel with a life-size picture of Ronald McDonald; a
whoopie cushion; an assortment of plastic beaks representing
bird species from around the globe; a green metallic top hat
with "Erin Go Bragh" embossed on the crown; three containers
of Silly Putty; a collection of matchbook-size Flags of All Nations (minus Britain, which had been appropriated for Austin's
hat); a pink plastic tiara; a platinum-blond wig; and, of course,
a rubber chicken.

The rubber chicken was my pride and joy. It was a good two feet long from beak to tailfeathers, made of a resilient rubber that managed to be both firm and clammy. It was a sickly yellowish-tan color, with detail work done in a brilliant hateful orange that resembled the powdered cheese in a macaroni-and-cheese mix. It was stippled all over with pinprick-size dimples. It had a vaguely anatomical gross pink thing hanging out of its beak. I adored it.

I rummaged through the toy bag, shut my eyes, and said a silent eenie-meenie-miney-moe to the gods of chance. My hand fell upon one of the plastic bird beaks. Perfect. I pulled out two beaks and offered them to Austin. "Flamingo or cormorant, my dear?"

"I'll take the flamingo, thank you," she replied. We strapped the beaks over our noses and turned to Annabelle, who was gazing at us with mild incredulity. "Is there a problem, young lady?" I asked.

"Nope," Annabelle replied. "No siree, bob. No problem at all."

"No problem at all . . . what?" Austin prompted.

"Oh, sorry. My abject apologies; I don't know what I was thinking. No problem at all, Mr. Big Enchilada; no problem at all, oh Great and Powerful Oz."

"That's better," I said. "But you still must be punished." I dove back into the toy bag and found the rubber chicken. Shielding it from Annabelle's view, I gestured to Austin with it. "Good heavens, Sophia," she said. "We've barely even started, and you want to bring on the pièce de résistance. Have a little self-control."

"Oh, all right," I sighed, putting the chicken back. "But we do have to punish her severely. Big Enchilada, I believe it's time for . . . The Tape."

Austin clutched her throat. "Not . . . The Tape!" she cried. "She's so young! She's barely thirty-four! You'll scar her for life!"

"Ha ha," I replied. "Now she'll learn not to meddle with Mr. Big Enchilada and The Great and Powerful Oz."

With a great show of fear and reluctance, Austin pulled the Leonard Nimoy tape and the Walkman out of the bag. "I hope you know what you're doing," she told me. She put the headphones on Annabelle, handed her the tape player, and, giving me one last, pleading look, pressed Play.

Annabelle kept a careful, even ostentatious straight face. The muffled strains of Leonard Nimoy leaked out from the headset, and Austin and I performed a few figures of the Mexican hat dance, stamping our feet and crying "Ole!" when the spirit moved us. Annabelle's straight-face efforts became rather more determined, but she kept her composure admirably.

"Okay, this is boring," I said at last, removing my cormorant beak and switching off the tape. "Let's do something else. Let's play pirates."

"Hey, I'm not done yet," Austin said. "I've got a lot of Mexican hat dancing to do before I die. Turn the tape back on."

"But I'm tired of being a cormorant," I whined. "I wanna play something else. Give me that beak."

"I'll give you the beak when I'm good and ready. If you want it, you'll have to pry it from my cold dead nose."

I began windmilling my fists and bouncing on the balls of my feet like (I hoped) Jack Dempsey. Austin responded in kind, and Annabelle egged us on shamelessly, batting her eyelashes when one of us made a particularly deft move.

By this time, a smallish crowd had begun to gather. The clean-up girl in the French maid's outfit kept glancing at us, and at the woman in the sling getting fisted, and back at us, and at the interrogation scene in the corner, and back at us again. The couple at the St. Andrew's cross had finished their flogging and were unabashedly staring and grinning. A tight knot of three very butch dykes were leaning against the wall a few feet away, playing it cool and pretending not to watch. I caught the eye of the cutest one and winked. She snorted and looked away.

Austin finally stopped, panting slightly. "A worthy opponent at last," she said. "Let us defer our dispute to a more suitable time. Anyway, I'm bored with the beak now. Why don't we change our names?"

"Good idea," I replied, tossing the beaks and the tape player back into the bag. "Okay, Annabelle. From now on, until I instruct you otherwise, you are to address me as . . . oh, let's see . . . the Grand High Muckety-Muck."

"And I," Austin said, "hereafter wish to be known as Captain Picard."

"Oh, please, no," Annabelle begged. "I can't call you Captain Picard. That would be blasphemy. My people would never forgive me."

I scowled. "Are you sassing us, young lady?"

She pondered the question carefully. "Well, yes, oh Grand High Muckety-Muck," she said at last. "You didn't tell me not to. You just said you were going to try to make me laugh, and if I did laugh, you'd hit me."

"Fair enough," I agreed. The toy bag was beckoning anyway, and I began to rummage again. I selected a rubber chicken, and once again I proffered it to Austin. "Not quite yet, I think," she said. "It's still a bit early. Once we bring it out, you know, there's no going back."

"I suppose you're right." I put the chicken back, took out the Flags of All Nations, and began inserting them into the tops of Annabelle's boots. "What do you want to do instead?"

"I think it's time for the humiliation and degradation portion of the evening. What do you think?"

"Excellent idea," I said. "Humiliation and degradation coming right up. Let me just finish up with these flags. What do you think we should call her first?"

"Oh, you know," Austin replied airily. "Bad names. Mean stuff. That sort of thing."

I rolled my eyes. "Great," I said. "Bad names. Mean stuff. That narrows it down a lot." I turned back to Annabelle, who was suppressing a chuckle.

"You . . . you bad person, you," I began. "You . . . you . . . oh, come on, Austin, help me out here."

Austin gamely chipped in. "You're a cad, that's what you are," she said. "A cad and a bounder, leading innocent girls astray, squandering the family fortune on loose women and games of chance and expensive imported chocolate. You ought to be ashamed of yourself."

"Scoundrel," I added.

"Profligate."

"Wretch."

"Riffraff."

"Ummm . . ." I taunted. "Oh, I dunno. Ratbag?"

"Ratbag?" Annabelle laughed. "Oh, please."

I sighed. "I knew I should have taken notes. Bugger-all. What we need is a thesaurus."

Austin grinned, reached into her smoking jacket, and pulled out a miniature copy of Roget's Thesaurus. "I thought this might come in handy."

I planted a giant wet kiss on Austin's cheek and snatched the thesaurus out of her hand. "Hang on," I told Annabelle, who was tapping her foot impatiently. "We'll be with you in a moment." I flipped through the book, quickly located the "bad names/mean stuff" section, and attacked Annabelle anew.

"Rogue."

"Rascal."

"Miscreant."

"Blackguard."

"Evildoer."

"Republican," Austin finished with a flourish.

"Bite me, Captain Picard," Annabelle retorted. "Call me anything you like, but Republican is below the belt. Besides, I am rubber and you are glue, and anything you say bounces off me and sticks to you." She blew a short, genteel raspberry.

"Am not," Austin replied. "Anyway, I'm tired of being called Captain Picard. From now on, I want you to address me as Queen of All She Surveys, Except for That Nasty Unswept Bit Over There in the Corner."

Annabelle snorted. She bit her lip, drew a breath, and snorted again. "Oh, God, I'm sorry." She giggled. Austin and I folded our arms across our chests and watched her sputter. "Odd, the things that set people off," Austin remarked. "It wasn't all that funny."

Eventually Annabelle's giggles died down. "Oops," she said. "I'm so sorry. I am but a simple country maiden and know little of your wicked big-city ways. Please forgive me."

Austin shook her head. "I think that was it. We've been very patient, but now she's got it coming to her. Bring it forth."

For the first time, Annabelle looked almost frightened. She peered anxiously as Austin and I dug into the toy bag with great determination.

Austin found the rubber chicken first.

She lifted it out of the bag, tenderly supporting its head and neck as I folded my hands and bowed. "Play ball," I said. Humming the chorus to "The Battle Hymn of the Republic," Austin slowly raised the chicken over her head.

Annabelle glared at the chicken. "You're kidding."

"Would we joke about a thing like this?" I said. "Bend over."

Annabelle gave us a pleading look, but I glowered ferociously and she bent over the table without a word. I grasped the chicken firmly by the neck. "How many? Fifty?"

"Fifty seems like a lot," said Austin. "How about twenty?"

"Twenty-five. And one to grow on and one for luck. Okay?"

Austin agreed, and I took careful aim and whacked Annabelle squarely on her butt. She let out an outraged yelp. "I think she's more frightened than hurt," Austin remarked.

"Not for long," I said. I gripped the chicken tighter and whacked Annabelle again and again, while Austin kept count in a thunderous bass voice. "Twenty-three . . . twenty-four . . . twenty-five!" she intoned.

"And one to grow on, and one for luck," I said, delivering two more hasty whacks. "Okay, you can stand up now."

Annabelle straightened and rubbed her butt. "God, you guys are weird," she said. "I mean . . . God, Grand High Mucky-Muck and Queen of—what was that again?—Queen of All She Surveys, Except for the Nasty Bit in the Corner. You guys are weird."

"We're not finished with you yet, young lady," I said. "No siree bob. Get down on your hands and knees."

She complied immediately. I selected a mint-flavored condom from a nearby safe-sex dish, tore it open with a flourish, and slowly drew it over the chicken's head and neck. The green condom produced a sickly, almost gangrenous look, the look of a chicken that hadn't been well for some time. "Why the condom?" Austin asked.

"Salmonella," I replied, handing her the chicken. "You can't be too careful. Would you do the honors?"

"I'd be delighted," she said. She placed the chicken between her legs, the head and neck dangling down obscenely. "Suck it, baby," she commanded. "Come on, suck it real good. Show me what you can do with that nasty mouth of yours. Suck my big chickeny dick."

Annabelle gave the chicken a repulsed look, then abruptly shook her head and grinned. She took a long, slow lick from the base of the neck all the way up to the tip of the beak. "Oh, it's so big," she breathed. "It's so big and juicy. It's huge, it's enormous, it's, it's . . . oh, hell, where's that damn thesaurus? Oh, fuck it, it's the biggest one I've ever seen. Give me that big hard chicken of yours. I want it all."

She slid the chicken head into her mouth, moving her lips up and down its neck, while Austin and I murmured encouragement. "That's it, baby. Take it all. You can do it. Lick the tip of the beak, yeah, that feels good. Now flick your tongue on that pink thing. Oh, that looks pretty. You're just a little slut, aren't you, can't get enough of that juicy drumstick. Come on, baste me with your steaming love juices. Show this big ol' rooster what you can do."

Austin began to move her hand in short, rapid motions up and down the chicken's neck. "I think I'm gonna come," she panted. "Oh, baby, don't stop. Oh God, that feels good. Oh . . . Oh . . . Oh . . . *brawwk!*"

The three of us collapsed into helpless giggles. The cleanup girl, who had been watching from the doorway for the last ten minutes, chuckled and rolled her eyes. The three butch dykes rolled their eyes and shrugged. The St. Andrew's cross couple applauded.

"This is no laughing matter," Austin said at last. "You think this is all a big joke, don't you? You young people these days don't take anything seriously."

"Now, Queen," I said. "She did an excellent job. Exceptional, in fact. I think she deserves some recognition, don't you?"

"Oh, definitely," Austin agreed. "She was fabulous. Bring on the awards stuff."

I dug into the toy bag one last time, and brought out the blond wig, the Erin Go Bragh hat, and the pink plastic tiara. I plopped the wig on my head, handed the hat to Austin, who scrunched it down over her black bowler, and placed the tiara on Annabelle's blond buzz cut. "Johnny, tell us about the prizes," I said.

I started humming "Pomp and Circumstance" while Austin went down on one knee. "For outstanding achievement in the field of comic sadomasochism and rubber-chicken blow jobs, we hereby confer upon Annabelle Hawkins the Most Distinguished Royal Trophy of the Imperial Chicken. Use it wisely." She handed the chicken to Annabelle.

Annabelle covered her face. "Aw, shucks," she said. "Thank you, my good people. I'd like to thank the Academy, the cast and crew, and all the little people who made me what I am today." She wiped away an imaginary tear and clutched the chicken to her breast.

"Is that it?" Austin said.

"That's it," I replied. I clapped Annabelle on the shoulder. "Okay. We're done now. Show's over. From now on, you are to address us as Austin and Sophia. Get dressed, and we'll get some wholesome snacks."

I picked up the toy bag, and the three of us strolled out of the dungeon and into the lounge. Annabelle picked up her dress from the clothes-check woman, who glanced at the rubber chicken and the bizarre headgear and gave us all a puzzled stare. Annabelle wriggled into her loose cotton shift and smiled at her sweetly. "I'm so proud," she said.

We sauntered over to the buffet table and started stuffing our faces. "Listen, Austin," I said, cantaloupe juice dripping down my chin. "We haven't done a historical scene in ages. How about the Medicis? You could be Pope Pius IV, and I could be Catherine de' Medici, and we could get some butchy artist type to be Michelangelo . . ."

Down in the Cinders

MARCY SHEINER

inderella sat by the hearth gazing with pride at the
excellent fire she had just built. She brushed her blond hair out
of her face, unmindful of the streaks of black soot left in the
wake of her hands. The flames licked at the perfect logs she had
herself chopped earlier in the day, their light and heat generat-
ing a similar feeling within Cinderella's body, which throbbed
as she anticipated the return of her stepmother and stepsisters.

This was her favorite time of day, dusk, the hour before
Brunhilde, Grunella, and Griselda finished the important work
they did out in the world and came home to be pampered by
Cinderella. She gazed around at the sparkling clean house,
fresh-cut flowers ornamenting every surface, pots bubbling on
the stove. As always, Cinderella derived great satisfaction from

her day's work; she loved creating a beautiful environment for herself and for others.

Especially for others.

She rose from the hearth, checked the soup, then headed out back with the laundry basket. It was a crisp autumn day, and the clothes she'd hung that morning were dry and sweet-smelling. Cinderella removed a pair of Griselda's panties from the line, buried her face in the crotch, and inhaled deeply. Before washing, the panties had reeked of her stepsister's hot musky juices; Cinderella had nearly fainted from the pungent aroma. But even without Griselda's juices encrusting the fine satin, the panties still gave Cinderella a thrill. Greedily she fingered the flimsy material, the little satin bow that rested just beneath her stepsister's navel, the filigreed lace that would caress Griselda's pearly thighs.

She became conscious of her own panties, their thin cotton graying from too many washings. The crotch was wet, as it usually was by evening. Though Cinderella felt ashamed of this, she simply couldn't help it. Her panties got wet when she scrubbed the floor. They got wet when she ironed her mother's skirts. They got wet when she made up her sisters' beds and fluffed their downy pillows. Serving her family made Cinderella so wet that sometimes she had to leave her chores, lie down among the cinders where she slept, and touch herself until she reached satisfaction. She had no idea what this was or why it happened, but she knew for sure it was wicked. Her stepmother had once caught her touching herself down there and had held her hands over hot coals until they blistered. Still, this did not stop Cinderella, it just made her more cautious.

She continued to remove the clothes from the line, pausing

to fondle a lacy bra cup, or to bury her face in a silk nightgown. Suddenly she heard the front door slam.

"I'm home!" shouted Brunhilde.

Cinderella threw the rest of the laundry into the basket and rushed to greet her stepmother in the foyer. Alas, she was too late. By the time she reached her, Brunhilde had removed her own coat and gloves. Cinderella dropped to her knees and kissed the hem of her stepmother's dress. "Forgive me, Mistress."

Brunhilde laughed wickedly, then tapped Cinderella on the shoulder with her walking stick. "Oh, nonsense, Cin, I don't know why you insist on this tedious scraping and bowing. Get up, you pathetic wretch! If you must abase yourself, at least put it to use. Fetch me a cup of mulled wine."

Cinderella scrambled to her feet, but not before bestowing a quick stealthy kiss on her stepmother's elegant fingertips. She raced into the kitchen and poured a cup of mulled wine, then brought it to Brunhilde, who had seated herself on the couch. She knelt and removed Brunhilde's high-laced boots, polished to a gleam just that morning by Cinderella herself. Brunhilde closed her eyes and leaned her head back, cradling her mulled wine while her stepdaughter massaged her feet.

"Mmm, that's a good girl," Brunhilde murmured, wiggling her elegant toes.

Cinderella's nipples instantly hardened. Suffused with shame, she leaned against her stepmother's legs and took a deep breath, trying to calm herself. Brunhilde kicked her away.

"Stop mooning, child! Your stepsisters will be home any minute, and you know how cross they get when you're unkempt. You look as if you've been lying in the cinders all day. Go wash your face."

"Yes, Mistress," Cinderella said, rushing off to wash her face and comb her hair.

When she returned, Grunella and Griselda had arrived home and were tossing their outerclothes all about the room, clamoring for their wine. Cinderella scrambled about gathering up gloves and hats and coats, then served them their wine and removed their boots. Unlike their mother, the girls did not compliment Cinderella on her foot massages, but kicked and cursed as she knelt before them. This only made her panties wetter and her nipples harder. When their mother wasn't looking, Cinderella surreptitiously took her sisters' toes into her mouth and sucked them. Grunella in particular had a way of maneuvering her foot that drove Cinderella to distraction. Grunella would slide her smooth delicate foot in and out of Cinderella's mouth, reaching all the way down her throat, then draw out and rub her toes along Cinderella's lips. Sometimes she'd pretend she was going to slide it in again, but just as Cinderella got ready to take it, Grunella would hastily withdraw, driving Cinderella wild with frustration. She swooned with pleasure whenever Grunella deigned to feed her an entire foot. The sensation of it against the back of her throat was exquisite, and she welcomed it as another opportunity to demonstrate her devotion.

"Cinderella!" shouted Brunhilde. "Where's supper?"

Cinderella hastened off to the kitchen. She served the family, jumping up every so often to fetch the salt, the cheese, a glass of water, hardly eating anything herself.

During supper the sisters spoke excitedly about a ball that was to be given by the prince of their province. It was rumored that the prince was seeking a wife, and the sisters hoped that one of them would be chosen.

Cinderella had known that eventually her stepsisters must marry, but she had not realized the time might come so soon. A sense of foreboding overcame her; feeling physically ill, she begged to be excused from her duties. She ran out to the field behind the house and, collapsing behind a large haystack, heaved great heart-heavy sobs. To think that her stepsisters might leave her! Never again to sniff Griselda's panties! Never again to suck Grunella's toes! Oh, she could not bear it. True, Brunhilde would still require her services, but Brunhilde was not as consciously cruel toward Cinderella as were her daughters.

Suddenly, out of nowhere, their next-door neighbor Fanny appeared.

"Child," she asked kindly, "why are you crying?"

"Be . . . because," gasped Cinderella between sobs, "my sisters are going to the ball to try and marry the prince."

Now, Fanny had been living next door to Cinderella and her family for years, and was constantly outraged by the way in which Cinderella was treated. Once or twice she had even said something to Brunhilde, who had told her in no uncertain terms to mind her own business. At last Fanny saw an opportunity to help Cinderella.

"Oh, my dear, you are so right to be upset. It's very unfair. But I'll tell you what: I will help you go to the ball."

Cinderella abruptly stopped crying and stared at Fanny. "Me? Go to the ball?"

Fanny clucked her tongue and stroked Cinderella's hair. "Oh, my poor sweet girl. You cannot imagine anything so wonderful for yourself, can you?"

Actually, Cinderella could not imagine anything so horrifying for herself. She was terrified of strangers; she hated leaving home; she fainted in large crowds. She shook her head, struck dumb by terror.

"Oh, yes, child, you can go! I will see to it. I shall make you the finest dress, buy you the finest shoes, fix your beautiful golden hair with my very own hands. Now, don't breathe a word of this to your mother or sisters. You just leave it all to Aunt Fanny."

As suddenly as she'd appeared, she vanished. Cinderella pulled herself together, dusted the hay from her dress, and slowly walked back to the house, hoping it had all been a bad dream.

If it was a dream, then the week was a nightmare. Fanny seized numerous opportunities to ambush Cinderella in the yard and measure her waist, her breasts, even her feet. Cinderella could not bring herself to hurt the woman's feelings, and so she suffered through these agonies, trying not to think about what would happen the night of the ball.

Meanwhile, the household was in a frenzy of preparations for Grunella and Griselda. Cinderella was busy sewing their gowns; many times a day she pricked her fingers, drawing blood, and would get so excited that she had to retire to the cinders to relieve herself.

The night of the ball Cinderella was in a state of rapture as she prepared and beautified her stepsisters. When she reddened Grunella's nipples with dye she'd made from berries, her sister shoved her mouth onto her full white breast, bidding her to suck. During Griselda's bath, she ordered Cinderella to rub the soap into previously forbidden crevices.

Flushed and happy, Cinderella arranged her stepsisters' hair into artful sculptures, and tenderly colored their beautiful faces. She all but forgot the purpose of these preparations, but when her sisters finally left, she remembered, and after Brunhilde retired, she crawled into the cinders to weep.

Suddenly she heard a knocking on the window.

"Psst! Cindy! Let me in!" It was that crazy Fanny—Cinderella had forgotten all about her. Quietly she crept outside.

Fanny held a blue gown resplendent with frills, puffy sleeves, and scalloped hem; Cinderella thought it wasn't half as elegant as the ones she'd fashioned for her stepsisters. In Fanny's other hand she held a pair of small glass slippers; again, they were no match for the white leather high-heeled boots Cinderella had lovingly selected to adorn her sisters' feet.

"Miss Fanny," she murmured, her head bowed respectfully, "you are very kind, but you see, I really don't want . . ."

"Nonsense, my child! Everything is arranged. My coachman will drive you and wait outside. If you don't show up by midnight, then he'll assume you've found yourself a more interesting chauffeur." She winked lasciviously and elbowed Cinderella in the ribs.

Resigned to her fate, Cinderella allowed Fanny to dress her in the ridiculous frilly gown and the tiny glass slippers. Although fairly certain that her stepsisters wouldn't recognize her in this getup, Cinderella kept a low profile at the ball. When she spotted Griselda and Grunella dancing with handsome young men, she seethed with jealousy. Strange images invaded her head, images of her stepsisters lying beneath these handsome men, squirming, writhing, letting them take their pleasure. Half crazed from jealousy and excitement, dazed and feverish, she suddenly found herself on the dance floor with none other than the prince himself.

He held her slim waist and steered her onto a darkened terrace.

"You," he murmured, gazing down at her upturned face, "are the most beautiful woman I have seen in my life. You are far more lovely than any other woman here."

Cinderella lowered her eyes, embarrassed. Obviously the man had not seen her stepsisters.

"And modest as well. I like that in a woman. I like you, sweetheart. In fact, I think I'm in love with you. I think I will choose you as my wife."

Cinderella was speechless.

"Ah, you're so happy you cannot speak. And well you should be. As my wife, you will have a dozen servants to fill your every need. I will pamper and spoil you. I will make love to you ever so gently."

He placed a hand on her breast and brushed her nipple with his thumb, his touch so tentative as to be almost nonexistent. Cinderella's nipple shriveled and receded. "I promise I shall never touch you any harder than that, my sweet princess." He slid his hand down her waist and rested it lightly on her hip, leaned forward and kissed her eyes, then her ears, gentle kisses that tickled the way a crawling insect might.

A wave of nausea engulfed Cinderella. She flashed on the memory of Grunella's foot prying her mouth open, moving relentlessly down her throat with no consideration or hesitancy. She marveled at how differently she responded to her stepsister than she did to the prince—he made her skin crawl.

Cinderella was shaken out of her musings by the sound of the clock striking midnight. "I must go!" she cried, terrified that she wouldn't reach Fanny's coachman in time and would be stuck with this simpering creature for the rest of the night. She jerked herself from his loose embrace and flew down the castle stairs. One of her slippers caught on a crack and fell off; Cinderella had no time to retrieve it. She rushed into the waiting coach, slammed the door, and said more forcefully than she'd said anything in her entire life, "Let's go!"

When she got home, Cinderella ran directly into the field, tore off her dress, and hid it behind the haystack. She went to the well and washed her face, trying to scrub off the prince's insipid touch.

"Ugh!" she said out loud. "I'm glad that's over!"

The next morning there was a great hubbub throughout the province. The prince ordered all houses searched for the beautiful girl who'd worn the glass slipper that had been left on his stairway after the ball. Three manservants arrived at Cinderella's home and demanded to see every female in the household.

Griselda and Grunella rushed right out and tried on the glass slipper, pushing and prodding their big feet this way and that—to no avail. Cinderella sat quaking behind the stove, hoping not to be seen, but eventually one of the manservants discovered her. She kicked and shrieked and bit his arm, but he dragged her out of hiding and forced her to try on the slipper, which, of course, fit perfectly.

Grunella and Griselda gasped. "How can this be?"

Cinderella, in a fit of tears, threw herself on Brunhilde. "I didn't want to go," she wailed. "Fanny made me do it. I'm so sorry. Please don't send me away." She crawled from Brunhilde to Griselda to Grunella, clutching at their hems, licking their boots in a frenzied display of groveling.

Meanwhile, the prince had arrived and saw the glass slipper sparkling on the foot of . . . a filthy wretch who crawled around the floor like a dog.

"How can this be?" he asked, appalled that he had pledged betrothal to this creature.

"Some terrible mistake," said Brunhilde, scooping Cinderella off the floor and holding her close. "She's very delicate, very excitable. I must put her to bed at once. Please go."

But the prince, accustomed to getting his way, was not to be put off.

"Madam," he said, folding his arms over his chest and pointing his chin in the air, "I have proposed marriage to your wretched daughter—and you can be sure I am a man of my word. You should be grateful that I am willing to take her off your hands."

"Oh, really?" Brunhilde said, drawing herself up to her full height, which made her a good four inches taller than the prince. "Well, young man, since you *are*, after all, the *prince*, and since you *are* a man of your *word*, then by all means, you *must* take Cinderella."

An ungodly wail ensued.

"Shh, child, it will be all right," Brunhilde whispered, patting Cinderella. "Trust me." To the prince she said, "Take her, but her sisters must come along and prepare her for the wedding ceremony. Cinderella is not strong enough to endure such a traumatic change without the support and guidance of her dear sisters."

"Yes," the sisters said in unison, "we must help prepare our dear sister for marriage."

The prince conferred with his manservants, who advised him to agree to Brunhilde's terms.

"Well, then," he said, looking with barely disguised loathing at his bride-to-be, "let's go."

At the prince's castle, Cinderella and her sisters were shown to a large chamber fit for a royal lady. The closets overflowed with colorful gowns, precious jewels, ornate headdresses, expensive perfumes. In the center of the room sat a large canopied bed. A chandelier hung from the ceiling, and beveled mirrors stood in every corner.

Cinderella watched in awe as her sisters swept quickly through the closets, pulling out dresses and crinolines. "No, no, these will never do," moaned Griselda. She called for a servant and demanded scissors, rope, and riding clothes. She sent for the stable boy and asked to see his collection of riding crops. She summoned the kitchen maid and had her deliver all manner of cooking utensils.

By evening Griselda and Grunella had adorned themselves from head to toe in leather. They'd dressed Cinderella in a tight corset, garters, stockings, and the infamous glass slippers. Several times the poor girl begged to be told what was going on; the sisters responded by feeding her a foot, or pinching her exposed nipples. By the time they sent a servant to fetch the prince, Cinderella was so wet and hot she'd lost all trepidation. "Trust us," whispered Griselda, and opened the door for Prince Charming.

"Wh . . . what?" he asked, stunned by the scene before him. The room glowed in candlelight. An ornate chandelier had been replaced with a large meathook from which a rope swayed hypnotically. The sisters looked as if they were on their way to hunt with the hounds. And his fiancée was spread out on the bed in her underwear. The prince covered his eyes discreetly.

Griselda locked the heavy wooden door. "Welcome, sweet prince," she said, savagely enunciating each syllable. "You are about to get more than you ever imagined when you chose Cinderella to be your loving princess."

The prince laughed to disguise his fear. Grunella cracked her riding crop across his calf. "Shut up, you idiot! Disrobe at once."

"Madam, I am your prince! How dare you—"

Another crack of the whip, this time from Griselda. "Disrobe! Now!"

Terrified, the prince did as he was told. To his dismay, when he removed his trousers a fully erect penis sprung forth.

The sisters cackled gaily. "Didn't I tell you, Grunny? Didn't I peg him?"

"Peg me?" asked the prince.

"A bottom," said Grunella, placing the handle of her whip beneath his penis and raising it for inspection. "Like our dear little sister."

All eyes turned to Cinderella. She was kneeling forward on her haunches, intently watching her sisters and the prince. Her breasts hung over the top of her corset, the nipples elongated. One had been pierced and fitted with a diamond-studded hoop. A gold chain dangled from her neck. Her hair had been plaited into dozens of tiny braids that swayed around her innocent face.

"Lovely, isn't she?" said Griselda.

When the prince made no reply, Griselda cracked her whip across his buttocks. "I said lovely, isn't she?"

"Y . . . yes," replied the prince.

"Oh, but *you* think she's beneath you! *You* think you're doing her—and us—a *favor* by 'keeping your word.' Ugh!" She flicked her whip across the prince's member. He jumped, but his prick grew half an inch.

"Our little sister," said Griselda, "is a precious treasure. You won't find the likes of her among your spoiled queens and princesses. Did you really think we'd give her up without a fight?"

Cinderella was amazed; never had she heard her sisters praise her. Hot liquid dribbled from between her legs and onto the sheets.

"Well, we won't give her up, not unless we deem you worthy."

"What must I do?" asked the prince, who'd begun unconsciously rubbing his member.

"Why, it's simple. You must learn how to treat Cinderella. How to keep her purring like a kitten." Griselda approached the bed, grabbed Cinderella's braids and yanked her head backwards. "*We* know how. We know all of her secrets, don't we, Cindy?" She stuck a finger into Cinderella's mouth. Cinderella closed her eyes and sucked. "We're perfectly willing to teach you, princey-poo. But only if you cooperate fully. Only if you trust us."

The prince, squeezing his scrotum absently, murmured, "I am your humble student."

"Good. Because we're going to teach you how to treat our sister in the manner to which she is accustomed. We're going to teach you to switch, to be a top for *her*, but you must remain subservient to *us*. Do you think you can do that?"

"I'll try," said the prince.

"I'll try, *Mistress*."

"I'll try, Mistress."

A million thoughts were swirling through Cinderella's head. Had her sisters known all these years the pleasure she derived from worshipping and serving them? Did they know about her wet panties, her sinful self-ministrations? Had their cruelty been deliberate? Had it been an act? She looked at Grunella, who seemed to read her mind.

"Oh, yes, Cinderella, we have always known your nature, and catered to it. But don't think we didn't derive as much pleasure as you. Griselda and I are natural-born tops. We love dominating. Of course," she giggled, "sometimes we had to restrain ourselves in front of mother."

"All right, all right," said Griselda impatiently. "Enough talking. Let's get on with it."

"Fine," said Grunella. "For now, Prince, you are to observe—just watch."

"May I touch myself, Mistress?"

"Excellent. Yes, you may touch yourself. In fact, it's mandatory." She turned to Cinderella. "On your feet."

Cinderella clambered out of bed. Griselda and Grunella quickly cuffed her hands behind her back, tied her ankles together, and clipped a chain to each nipple. "Walk," they ordered, each one pulling a nipple chain.

Cinderella teetered after her sisters, tits-first. By the time they reached the hanging rope, her thighs were drenched with her own juices. Griselda slid a hand between her legs, extracted some of the wetness, and shoved a finger into the prince's mouth.

"See what a little slut she is? Humiliation makes her cream. Doesn't it, Cindy?"

Cinderella moaned.

"On your knees, bitch." Cinderella sank to her knees. Grunella lifted her leather skirt. "Lick."

Cinderella avidly licked her sister's clitoris and labia, then snaked her tongue up inside her. Grunella grabbed her head and pressed it firmly against her while she ground her hips.

"Okay, that's enough pussying around," said Griselda, pulling Cinderella by the hair and forcing her to stand. "Let's give her what she really wants—what we could never do at home."

With the rope she tied Cinderella to a large cross-shaped object she'd found in the stable. It was held up by the meathook, so Cinderella was hanging slightly above her sisters, who stood on either side and raised their whips. Cinderella's eyes hungrily drank in their beauty as they stood before her in their leather riding clothes, their long hair flowing behind them. She reveled in the feeling of being the object of their focused attention. Slowly they brought the whips down on either of her thighs.

As much as her stepsisters had humiliated her, never before had they struck Cinderella. Something deep inside her leaped out to greet the blows, and she realized she had been wanting this for a long, long time. Each crack of the whip provided Cinderella another chance to show her sisters how much she adored them. The more it hurt, the more it proved her love.

With great joy Cinderella received the blows, glad there was someone to witness her surrender.

The sisters whipped her belly, her back, even her breasts and vagina. As their blows got progressively harder, their excitement mounted. Their eyes became molten; a vein throbbed in Griselda's temple; sweat dripped down Grunella's face.

"Oh yes," they murmured, "she likes being beaten, don't you, Cindy?"

"Yes." The more excited they became, the more Cinderella wanted them to hurt her. She arched her back, her body virtually kissing the whip. She watched the prince cupping his balls and pulling on his thick cock. Saliva trickled from his mouth. The sisters followed Cinderella's gaze.

"Ah, yes, see how hard he is. See how his muscles bulge. The weaker you get, the stronger he becomes."

It was true; the prince was being transformed from the fawning creature who had danced with her into a strong, powerful man who could provide the hardness she so badly needed. If her surrender had the power to strengthen him this way, gladly she would yield.

"Shall we stop?" teased Griselda.

"No, please, no." Cinderella sensed that if the sisters continued, she would be taken beyond her conscious thoughts and into the realm of pure sensation. That was where Cinderella wanted to go. That was what she'd been striving for all her life.

"But Cinderella, you have marks on your skin," taunted Griselda. "Soon you may bleed."

"Don't stop," Cinderella repeated. "Please don't stop."

"Good God, don't stop," shouted the prince.

The sisters laughed and resumed their whipping. When Cinderella was nearly fainting, they untied the ropes and lowered her to the floor. "Go," ordered Griselda. "Go suck your husband's cock."

Cinderella crawled across the floor. The prince towered over her, and with no hesitation thrust his member between her parted lips.

"Suck it, you whore. Worship my royal prick."

Cinderella's flesh felt as supple as well-worn leather. Her mouth, cunt, and anus ached to be filled. Her heart palpitated with love and generosity; she wanted to serve; she wanted to give pleasure.

"Lick your husband's balls," said Grunella, and Cinderella gratefully lowered her mouth to the hanging sacs, tenderly rolling each by turn in her mouth. With one hand she stroked the prince's member and with the other prodded his anus. The prince groaned and grabbed her by the nape of her neck, his touch that of a man taking possession. In that moment Cinderella knew she had been given over to a new master. Eager to prove herself worthy, she grasped his prick and lovingly rubbed it all over her face, in her eyes, over her cheeks. A drop of milky white fluid shimmered on the head; Cinderella licked it off, savoring its salty taste.

"Drink my royal nectar," whispered the prince. "Swallow my precious fluid."

"Oh, yes," gasped Cinderella. "Anoint me." She sucked and licked and stroked until the prince released his semen and flooded her open mouth. She gulped it down.

Griselda had attached some kind of penis-shaped piece of leather onto herself with a belt. She kneeled behind Cinderella and thrust the makeshift prick into the girl's sopping hole. Grunella fastened her clit onto the prince's mouth, and ordered him to lick.

Cinderella's cunt closed gratefully around whatever was inside it. She continued to lick and kiss her husband's balls and prick while Griselda pounded into her. She pressed a finger to the little button she'd discovered between her legs, and soon her whole body was climbing. She pressed and bucked and reached for whatever was coming, and suddenly felt it: an explosion of a magnitude that she had never experienced in her playful little games among the cinders. Rather than just a little tremor between her legs, her entire body seemed to open and contract. Her cunt sucked on Griselda's strange appendage, and a loud moan escaped her lips, muffled by the prince's semi-erect member. She raised up her hips so Griselda could thrust even deeper, creating new waves of ecstasy deep inside her. Griselda squeezed Cinderella's buttocks and slid a finger into her anus. Behind her closed eyelids Cinderella saw an explosion of color and light. As the contractions in her body subsided, the light burst into fragments like shooting stars, and then funny little pictures of people and animals danced behind her lids. As if from a great distance, she heard her sisters grunting; they, too, were experiencing ecstatic release.

"You see," Griselda quietly told the prince after a few moments, "keeping Cinderella takes a lot of work." She flexed her bicep.

The prince gazed down at the blond head resting on his thigh, the small delicate hand cradling his balls.

"I intend to make it my life's mission," he said.

Cinderella raised her head and kissed her fiancé. Then she kissed each of her sisters.

"Don't worry," said Griselda, "we'll check in regularly in case you need a refresher course."

"Oh," said the prince, "I'm quite sure that I will."

The Littlest Dominatrix

LISA MONTANARELLI

She was twenty-one and stunned when she found that corporate executives would pay $200 an hour to chew on her used underwear or have her dress them in lacy panties. Stay calm and get the cash upfront, she told herself, making this her mantra as they handed her stacks of newly minted twenty-dollar bills, stiff and crisp as sandpaper, and stuck together so she had to take extra care in counting them.

Her last job had been phone domination. She'd worked downtown in one of those cheaply renovated buildings, where the gray-beige walls left a cardboard taste in her mouth and the industrial carpet scraped and prickled her feet like beard stubble when she kicked off her flip-flops in the summer.

The phone-domination office was a casual place. The girls

dressed in sweats like strippers on their way home from work. And some of them were strippers, but not Betsy. She'd found this gig combing the want ads for something to help pay for school. She thought she was answering an ad for a boring tele-marketing job, but before she knew it, she was talking to men who dialed 1-900-YO-BITCH—a boldface number on a back-page newsprint ad, featuring the image of a domina with prowling eyes and plastic tits licking her lips. She looked vaguely like some airbrushed supermodel whose name Betsy couldn't recall, but nothing like Betsy or any of the girls who actually worked there.

This didn't matter. The callers never learned that Betsy was a long-faced, flat-chested girl who tied her hair back in a per-petual ponytail and wore hooded sweatshirts and flip-flops to work. And they never found out that her name was Betsy. They spoke to Tatiana the Phone Mistress, clad in a black leather corset and thigh-high boots with stiletto heels, though some-times she sprouted a green mohawk and donned nose piercings and steel-toed army surplus boots, or even snowshoes or flip-pers on an especially creative day. Almost all the callers were male. Most of them wanted Betsy—or Tatiana—to chain them verbally to a St. Andrew's cross, tie up their cock and balls, and whale on them with straps, paddles, floggers, singletails, and occasionally even coat hangers or cattle prods.

Betsy had her own small cubicle, but voices carried through the thin walls, and she wondered what the whips-and-chains callers thought when they overheard the other phone-dominas bark "Lick that snowshoe, slut!" or "You're really going to get it when Dad gets home!" or "Get back in your prison cell, les-bian jailbait!" A number of callers longed to be locked in a lesbian-only prison. Where were they getting this idea? Was it some new TV show? Betsy didn't think there was such a thing as a lesbian-only prison, but she was willing to play a guard or fellow inmate and keep such insights to herself.

Her favorite role was the evil serpent lady who lurked in the shallow waters off a deserted island and snacked on the private parts of unsuspecting shipwrecked sailors as they swam for shore. This was more fun in retrospect. The call had lasted two hours. The metal folding chair was digging twin points of bone-bruise in her butt, and the caller had already come once when she uttered the words "private parts." But the high-pitched nasal voice kept insisting, "A huge galleon is sinking! What are you going to do with all those seamen, clinging to crates on the surf?" He actually talked this way, and Betsy didn't know what to do. Finally she invited her posse of man-eating, amphibian sea-monster gals for a beach barbecue with testes flambé. At the phrase "testes flambé," he emitted a muf-fled "Umpf" and hung up.

It was a slow Monday night, and the phone-domme next door craned her head around the partition separating their cu-bicles. "You are so gifted." She enunciated each word, tossing blond ringlets out of her face.

Gifted? Was she serious? She sounded more like Betsy's high school teacher than someone her own age.

"I'm Skyrockets."

"You're what?" Betsy smothered a laugh as she realized this was the girl's name. "I'm Tatiana, but my real name's Betsy. What's yours?"

Skyrockets Ludlow was, in fact, her given name, the name on her driver's license. Her parents had chosen this moniker on an afternoon of tearful synergistic bliss, when her mother had given birth in the living room of their Santa Cruz condo. It was 1976. "Skyrockets in flight! Afternoon Delight!" had just been released and came bouncing out of the radio as the baby's bald noggin squeezed through the birth canal and again as the midwife dangled her upside down by the heel and spanked her. Betsy had grown up in San Francisco, but even she didn't know anyone named Skyrockets. She thought the name verged on child abuse, but Skyrockets said her folks were totally hip and groovy, and besides, she was a lot better off than her sister, Starry Nipples. If only they'd rebelled against their parents and changed their names to Phallic Warhead and Tit Implants.

Skyrockets had recently moved from Taos, New Mexico, where she'd studied Tantra at a commune till the guru and his wives hightailed it for the border on charges of tax evasion. Betsy knew Tantra had something to do with sex, but not exactly what. This was something she ought to know. On the way home from her shift, she wandered into an Internet café and shelled out a few bucks to use a computer. But in half an hour of Web surfing, all she could figure out was that Tantra had to do with sex, Hinduism, Buddhism, Sanskrit, more sex, meditation, and yoga.

As it happened, Skyrockets did some domination in person as well, and she wanted Betsy's help with a client who sometimes got out of hand.

"He's the sweetest man," she said, "a former Navy football player who's into forced feminization and slut training. The thing is, he has this lifelong fantasy of cross-dressing in public, and I just don't think I can handle him by myself."

It wasn't simply a matter of cross-dressing in public.

George, also known as Liona, wanted to be forced into slutty lingerie and taken shopping. He wanted Skyrockets to escort him, preferably in light bondage, into the stall of a women's dressing room, where she would coerce him into trying on pretty panties and, ideally, servicing unsuspecting shoppers who strolled into the dressing room to try on clothes. He admitted, sadly, that this last part with the shoppers might be a bit unrealistic.

"He's offered twelve hundred dollars," said Skyrockets, "but I don't want to do it alone. I'll give you four hundred just to come with me. It'll take three hours max, and you'll barely have to do a thing. Besides, it'll be a learning experience. You can look at it as a kind of training."

Betsy hesitated. She was a little late with her rent on the roach-infested apartment she shared with three friends from high school. But the whole thing sounded rather risky. First, there was the problem of taking a guy into the women's dressing room. The staff would object, especially if they seemed to be forcing him in there.

She shook her head. "I'd like to, but I don't think it'll work."

"I didn't think it would either," said Skyrockets, "but then I found the perfect place."

The perfect place was Ross Dress for Less. Known to the locals as Cross Dress for Less, it carried large sizes at cheap prices and was a favorite shopping haunt for cross-dressers, trannies, and drag queens.

"They're used to this sort of thing," Skyrockets said. "They see guys in dresses all the time."

"But not in the women's dressing room."

"We'll just tell them George is transsexual. Trust me, it'll work."

That Saturday Betsy took the bus over to Skyrockets's apartment an hour before George showed up. Since she'd only done phone domination, she didn't have anything to wear. She could borrow Skyrockets's leathers, but she'd have to bring her own shoes. She chose her two-inch black pumps—*sensible shoes*, her mother called them.

Skyrockets answered the door in her bathrobe, and Betsy's eyes went wide as she walked in. The place was a real hippie pad with incense burning and Indian print gauze billowing from the ceiling. And what was that smell? Patchouli.

In the bedroom, Skyrockets had Betsy try on a few different outfits before she decided on a black leather shirt—a bit baggy in the bust—and a matching skirt that came down to her knees. Skyrockets herself squeezed into a black leather mini-skirt and talked Betsy through the ordeal of lacing her corset. She put on mascara, eyeliner, vamp lipstick, and six-inch-heeled thigh-high boots. When Betsy suggested they tone it down to be discreet, she added a black leather jacket to cover her cleavage.

At five past two, the doorbell rang. Skyrockets was still glued to the bathroom mirror. "Can you get that?" she asked, fussing with her makeup.

Betsy opened the door and took a step back. The man's chest spanned the entire door frame. She barely came up to his sternum. His massive chin and jaw blocked her view of his face.

"I'm George. You must be Tatiana." He ducked under the

door and lumbered over to the couch, whose springs let out a cry of alarm under his weight.

"I brought my own things," he said, displaying a navy blue duffel bag that looked like a toy purse in his hands. He was a towheaded man with kind eyes and a sweet smile, but his palms and forearms were grease-stained, and there was black grit around his cuticles and under his nails. His fingers were as broad as Betsy's big toes, and they were quaking in anticipation.

Betsy's throat clenched up. Stay calm, she told herself, wondering how she got herself into this. What was Skyrockets thinking?

"My ex bought these for me," he said. "I have a hard time getting this kind of stuff for myself without encouragement."

She felt a rush of sadness as he unzipped the duffel bag with shaking fingers and held up a slinky gold lamé dress, big as a tablecloth, and a pair of size-sixteen gold stiletto heels. He looked at her, as though guessing her thoughts, and shrugged. "I'll never be a girly girl," he said.

Skyrockets strutted in on six-inch heels, wielding a riding crop.

"George! Good to see you!" she shrieked, thrusting her butt out as she leaned over and hugged him. "What have you done to your hands?"

"My car broke down yesterday, and I got out and popped the hood . . . I wasn't thinking . . . Sorry, Mistress. I scrubbed them with Mechanics Hand Cleaner, but it just won't come off." He bowed his big head.

Skyrockets stood erect, hands on her hips. "What a bad little sissy—always making things difficult!"

"I brought you something." He fetched a fat white envelope out of his duffel bag. Skyrockets tore it open and counted the worn, rumpled bills. Betsy tried not to stare, but she'd never seen such a thick wad of cash.

"Now get dressed," Skyrockets said. "Show Tatiana what you learned recently." She shook her crop at him.

"Yes, Mistress." George pulled off his T-shirt and stepped out of his pants and boxers. With tube socks still on his feet, he lay down on his back and fumbled with his balls. Betsy gave Skyrockets a quizzical look.

"He's pushing his testes into his groin," she explained, looming over him.

When he finished, he fished in his duffel bag and pulled out some scissors and what looked like surgical tape.

Betsy looked away, feeling woozy. "I don't think I can watch this. Blood makes me faint."

"What do you mean, blood?" asked Skyrockets, as George folded his empty scrotum around his penis. With the scissors, he snipped off a five-inch piece of surgical tape and taped the whole package, which looked like a hotdog in a bun, between his legs where his pussy would have been. He then pulled on a pair of lacy black panties. Betsy had never seen anything like this. It was half medical procedure, half fashion show. And he was still wearing tube socks.

"Good sissy!" said Skyrockets.

He smiled and stuck his big arms through the straps of a massive bra, but he couldn't reach around his back to fasten it.

Skyrockets sputtered in frustration. "After all that, you'd think she'd know how to put on a bra!" She turned to Betsy. "Would you please show *her* the right way to do it? You're Liona the slave-girl now," she said, whacking Liona on the butt. "And take off those damned socks!"

Making a mental note to think of George as a *she* from now on, Betsy helped Liona out of *her* bra and showed *her* how to pull it around *her* waist like a belt, fasten it in front, then turn it around so the cups were in front and the clasp in back. Liona took some foam wedges out of her duffel bag and inserted them in the cups. Suddenly she had rocket tits (which helped dispel the pronoun confusion). She shimmied into the gold lamé dress—with Skyrockets striking her with the crop whenever she made a less-than-dainty gesture. A gold lamé strap snapped as she stretched it over her shoulder, and she looked *très déshabillé* as she bent over for a spanking.

When Liona finished dressing, Skyrockets went to the bathroom to fetch some makeup. Betsy followed her, and as soon as they were out of earshot, she whispered, "They'll never let us in the women's dressing room. This is crazy."

But Skyrockets wouldn't even look her in the eye. She plucked her makeup case off the bathroom sink. "Trust me. I know what I'm doing."

Liona got the same vamp lipstick as Skyrockets and Betsy. Then came false eyelashes and a Farrah Fawcett wig. She squeezed her feet into the gold stilettos. Then, rocketing up to her full seven-foot height, she paraded around the room, swaying her lubricated hips and ducking around the light fixture on the ceiling. Betsy kept waiting for the heels to snap in half, but she had to admit, Liona looked *good*, and she walked better in stilettos than Skyrockets did.

But there was still the problem of getting her into the women's dressing room. Liona was the biggest drag queen

Betsy had ever seen, but she didn't look like she lived full-time as a woman. Betsy had very limited experience with male-to-female transsexuals, but she was beginning to think she might know a bit more than Skyrockets did.

Skyrockets was shaking her crop, running after Liona like an elephant trainer. "You can't go out in public like that!" she shrieked. "We have to do something with those hands. Put your hands on the kitchen table." She handed Betsy some blood-red nail polish.

Bending over, Liona splayed her cigar-fingers on the table and wriggled her butt. Betsy tried to paint her nails, but Liona kept flinching because Skyrockets was caning her thighs, and by the time Betsy finished, Liona had the claws of a griffin or Sphinx, crossed with a Jackson Pollock painting.

Skyrockets stepped back and gave her the once-over. "Your nails can dry in the car," she said.

They piled into the 1988 Honda Civic that Skyrockets had bought at the Tantra commune in Taos. Liona, ballooning in the passenger seat, fanned her art moderne paws out the window to dry. She glanced over her shoulder at Betsy and batted her eyelashes.

"Skyrockets probably warned you: I really lose it in the intimate apparel section. I don't know what comes over me."

"That's why Tatiana's here," said Skyrockets. "She has a black belt in jujitsu."

"I do not!" said Betsy, kicking the back of her seat, as they almost sideswiped a bus.

Ross Dress for Less was the size of a high school gymnasium with hospital-white walls and a low ceiling. It was a hot August day, and the store sizzled with excited, sweaty shoppers. As they promenaded through the automatic double glass doors, it struck Betsy how odd they looked, showing up in the middle of the afternoon in black leather and vamp lipstick with a gold-lamé Arnold Schwarzenegger, with Farrah Fawcett hair, swelling over the cashiers and clothes racks like a balloon in the Macy's Parade.

When they hit Women's World, Liona uttered a high-pitched swooning cry. All three hundred slinky gold-lamé pounds of her soared—borne by invisible shopping-attendant angels—toward the intimate apparel shop. Her tiny shoulder-strap purse sailed on the air in her wake. Customers, rifling through the racks, froze and stared. Skyrockets tottered after her, flapping her arms by her shoulders like a black leather flamingo trying to fly. And Betsy scurried after them, though she couldn't keep up with them, even in her *sensible* two-inch heels.

She found them alone in an aisle of lacy panties—Liona towering above Skyrockets, but quivering. "Sorry, Mistress, I just can't help myself. Ow!" Skyrockets lifted her gold lamé skirt and pinched her.

Liona did not exactly "shop" for lingerie. She snatched things off the racks as if her life depended on it. Soon she was clutching an armload of lingerie and counting the individual pieces. There were eight pairs of lacy panties and five XXXL fishnet bodystockings in black, gold, orange, silver, and bronze. She stopped at the shoe rack to pick out a few pairs of stiletto pumps, then bolted for the dressing room. Skyrockets ran after her, shouting threats and (to Betsy's horror) brandishing the riding crop, which she must have smuggled into the store under her leather jacket. But Liona ran with an almost supernatural energy. She was an athlete, and her endless legs took one stride for every two of theirs.

Betsy crept along behind them, sidling up to the racks of dark-colored garments, hoping they would camouflage her. She arrived just in time to see Liona on tiptoe, trying to slip the whole Farrah Fawcett–haired hulk of herself unseen into the ladies' dressing room.

She was almost inside, when a saleswoman with a hooked nose and gravity-defying hair came up behind her. "Excuse me, *sir*, but this dressing room is for women only."

Liona turned, her face flushing bright red. Her eyebrows stood out like white caterpillars.

Just then, as Liona and the saleslady faced off on the threshold to the holy land, a lithe gender-ambiguous personage— perhaps transsexual, but who could tell?—sashayed out of the dressing room with rhinestone-studded evening gowns tossed over her shoulder. She was clearly slumming at Ross, or perhaps they paid her to try on their clothes. She paused in the doorway, glanced at Liona, and walked off with a smirk.

Liona shrank and stumbled a bit, as if the invisible shopping angels, who had buoyed her up all this time, had let go and left her hanging in midair. Betsy crouched beside a circular garment rack. She had never seen a football player wither. She had to do something, but what?

The saleswoman took a step toward Liona. "Why . . . you have soot all over your hands! Why don't you give me those, and I'll show you where the men's dressing room is, okay?" She laid a hand on one of the hangers Liona was holding.

But Liona clutched her lingerie to her foam-wedge breasts. "No," she said.

The woman took a startled step back. "Well, I'll have to call security then."

Here we go, thought Betsy. She backed into the clothes rack till she was stooping in the center, surrounded by forest green jumpsuits. She and her brother used to hide like this as kids, when their mom took them shopping. There was nowhere comfortable to sit, so she squatted in her leather skirt and peered out between the jumpsuits, waiting for security to show up.

Suddenly Skyrockets barged between Liona and the saleslady. She was still holding the riding crop, but, thankfully, not brandishing it.

"What do you think you're doing? This is my sister!" she said, spraying *s*'s in the woman's face. "She just started living as a woman twenty-four-seven, and she has nothing to wear but the clothes on her back! Don't you see, this is the only place she can buy clothes to wear on the street!"

The saleslady looked at Liona with her armful of lacy panties, stilettos, and fishnet bodystockings. She shook her head. Inside the garment rack, Betsy was grinding her teeth, waiting for the guards to cart them off—perhaps to some lesbian-only prison. It occurred to her that if this were a horror movie, Skyrockets would be dead by now, for sure.

Then Skyrockets choked at bit, and Betsy saw she was weeping—big, lumpy, mascara-stained tears. How did she make herself cry like that?

"I am proud of my transsexual sister!" she shouted with all the PC moral indignation she could muster. Her words echoed through the store. Everyone turned and stared.

The dressing room was not far from the women's shoe racks, where two male-to-female transsexuals, dressed in sweatshirts and jeans, were trying on Reeboks, Nikes, and other *sensible* shoes. Their eyes riveted on Liona. Though Betsy had limited experience with MTFs, she was sure that these two had been living as women for a while, and it would be clear to them that Liona, in her Farrah Fawcett wig, slinky dress, and stiletto heels, had not. Would they think Skyrockets and Liona were making fun of them?

She crept toward the dressing room, where Skyrockets was still sobbing and carrying on. A crowd had gathered, and the saleslady was still studying Liona in her skimpy gold lamé "street clothes" and Skyrockets with her vamp lipstick, corset, and crop, and shaking her head. Betsy came up behind the saleswoman and tried to catch Skyrockets's eye. Finally she waved her arms, flagging her down. When Skyrockets glanced up, bleary eyed, Betsy pointed to the shoe racks and mouthed, There Are Real Transsexuals Over There and You Are Offending Them. Skyrockets looked over in the direction she was pointing, but by that time the two MTFs had joined the crowd and were pointing at them—at Betsy and Skyrockets—and they were laughing and tittering. Was everyone laughing at them?

Then Betsy noticed that Liona was chatting with a couple of attractive middle-aged women, and she looked less deflated. Her eyes sparkled, and as she showed them her panties and bodystockings, she fluttered her false eyelashes and even curtseyed.

The saleswoman walked off with Skyrockets stalking after her. "I want to speak to your supervisor!" she hollered. The crowd fizzled. A few people trailed Skyrockets, but most rolled their eyes at each other and went back to the racks.

Betsy sat down on the floor and pulled off her shoes. Her feet ached—and stank. She was sweating heavily. Her slimy stockings clung to her toes, and the leather shirt and skirt stuck to her armpits and thighs. Skyrockets was a drama queen, but at least she'd intervened, while Betsy hid in the garment rack cowering.

She looked around for Liona, who seemed to have vanished. But where would she have gone? Betsy checked the women's dressing room. It seemed empty. Perhaps everyone had left to see what the fuss was about. Then, way in the back, she heard some whacks and muffled screams. She recalled the *unrealistic* part of Liona's fantasy—how she wanted to service unsuspecting shoppers who came into the dressing room to try on clothes. Betsy turned to leave, then, thinking of the lesbian-only prison scenes her phone clients were always requesting, she paused and stood in the doorway. A woman ambled toward her with flowery blouses folded over her arm.

"Excuse me. Is this the ladies' dressing room?"

"Yes, but you can't go in right now. It's closed."

The woman eyed her curiously and walked away.

Duplicity

From *I Was a Teenage Dominatrix*

SHAWNA KENNEY

I loved to get lobbyists and lawyers. They seemed to know they were everyday assholes, and I tormented them for all the sexual harassment scenarios and male-chauvinistic behavior I imagined them to be a part of. My anger with them was sincere. They were the type of jerks my mom had to fetch coffee and type her fingers to the bone for—the kind I despised the most. Their snobby attitudes, their midlife-crisis sportscars, their decaying bodies, their bad comb-over hairdos. I couldn't imagine anyone falling in love with or wanting them sexually. I truly hated every inch of this type of man, and it paid off. They loved me for it.

* * *

One of my first out-calls was a cross-dresser way out in the sub-urbs of northern Virginia. I arrived at a small town house and a short, well-dressed Latin man who looked strangely feminine opened the door. He invited me in in broken English. Now, I could see he was wearing a light pink lip gloss and false eye-lashes. I told him I'd be in the bathroom changing, and or-dered him to strip and wait on his knees, just as Miranda taught me, and as I did with all of my clients. He just stared at me, standing in the middle of a plush, white square of carpet, surrounded by shelves of books and those enviable knickknacks of the well-traveled.

"Didn't you hear me? I said strip and get on your knees!" I knew Tony was listening at the door for the first few minutes, just to be sure everything went okay. If this jerk tried anything funny, his door would be knocked down in two seconds flat.

"Pu . . . pu . . . please, madam. I don't want to do that."

"I don't care what you *want*. I am the dominatrix and you'll do as I say!" I was on my period, and believe me, there's noth-ing scarier than a dominatrix with cramps. I must have sounded especially evil. Tears formed in his eyes.

"What's wrong?" I softened my tone. I didn't think he was dangerous anymore. Hopefully Tony got the same feeling.

"I just want to talk and be with you." The man offered me a seat on the couch. "May I take off my shirt?" he asked timidly.

"Go ahead."

He unbuttoned his white shirt to reveal a white corset that looked like it had seen better days—and even then, it was probably still ugly. He stared at me, as if to ask "Is this okay?" I nodded. He unbuttoned his pants. He had on the biggest grandma-looking underwear I'd ever seen. He looked down, ashamed.

"Does this o . . . o . . . offend you, Mistress?"

"No, why would it?"

He walked over to me and asked permission to lie on the couch, his head face up in my lap. I granted it, and we talked this way for the next two hours. I decided to test my third-year Spanish skills and he was thrilled with my clumsy efforts. "Diga me en Espanol," I told him. He said he was a surgeon, originally from Argentina. His wife knew about his love for women's clothing but didn't wish to see it. He spoke too quickly and I told him to slow it down, laughing to myself as I wondered why we never learned vocabulary like "cross-dresser," "submissive," or "you need to get some better underwear" in class. Whatever would Professora Maria Helena have thought of how I was implementing her lessons? I stroked his hair and told him of the other men I met like him, and he couldn't believe it.

"You mean, there are others?" The fifty-year-old became a child, his brown eyes big with joy and wonder.

"Of course." I told him about the special closet at Miranda's dungeon, filled with furs, silky dresses, nighties, shoes, and wigs for our cross-dressers. He was in complete shock.

"I come from a country where it is very important to be macho. To be like me is a disgrace."

"You are not a disgrace," I told him. "You are just you." It sounded weak when I said it, but it seemed to satisfy him. My friends always told me I should be a therapist—that or a bartender. How sad, I thought, not to be able to be yourself with your lover. I wondered if his visit with me made him feel better or worse. Better for finding someone who understands, or worse and frustrated for doing this behind his wife's back, suppressing his urges around her. Maybe it's no worse than some of my friends not knowing "the real me" and what I've done in the past. People can be judgmental, so we have to keep our secrets. We said pleasant good-byes and he told me he'd call the agency when he needed to talk again. The day was a lesson to me—every session was different because each person was different. "You are the dominatrix and you can do whatever you want." Miranda's words echoed in my head. True, but I could not continue to go through the motions of spanking and giving orders in the same way to every client. I had to pay attention, and tailor each session to fit the person I was with. I had to get creative. Just like with school and life in general, I wanted to push myself to do the best I could.

About twenty-five percent of all calls were out-calls. They opened up worlds I'd never seen up close. I was going to the finest hotels in Washington. Marble staircases. Glass elevators. If I'd had a particularly hectic day and no time to eat a decent meal, I'd have the guys order room service in time for our session. Shrimp, cheesecake, salad. It was the first time I could look at expensive menus and order exactly what I wanted with no thought of price. In true white-trash fashion I even ordered extra appetizers and desserts—food I knew I couldn't finish—and took it home with me for the next day. The client never seemed to care. Half the time it was on his company's credit card anyway.

I also got to explore some of the nicest homes. Houses you'd see in magazines. I had never been so close to such extreme wealth. Many rich older people lived alone in huge

mansions, with their pets as their only company. They just indulged their fantasies once in a while by paying someone like
me. It was always riskier going to someone's house. I mean,
who knew what they had planned? But I had Tony as backup,
plus I liked meeting them in their own surroundings. Studying their books. Pianos. Closets. Medicine cabinets. (Oh, the
medicine cabinets! I never realized what a medicated society
we lived in until I started this form of snooping! Anal-itch
cream. Antifungal ointment. Flush-free niacin. What is that
stuff?) Anyway, I think most were just plain lonely. Maybe
even bored with life. I showed up at one guy's house on a beautiful summer afternoon. I don't know if he even knew what a
dominatrix was or what, but he seemed extremely happy to
see me. He introduced himself as Norman, welcomed me in,
and asked me to please have a seat on the couch. He fixed me a
glass of ice water at my request, then sat down and put his face
in his hands.

"You don't have to get undressed or anything. I don't know
why I called you people," he said.

"I wouldn't be getting undressed anyway," I tried to explain to him. "I'm here to . . ." All of a sudden he was crying.
Big tears rolling over his thin, aging hands.

"My wife died twelve years ago," he sobbed. "And I haven't
been this close to a woman since." His chest heaved, he was
crying so hard by this time. I was completely stunned. I hadn't
prepared for this. He went on, "I don't know why I called. I
just wanted to talk to somebody—a woman."

I thought maybe he was getting some bright idea that I was
a prostitute, so I clarified that he was not going to have sex
with me or any such thing. He sobbed harder. It wasn't what

he wanted anyway. He really just wanted to talk. When I finally believed him, I put my hand on his back and smoothed
over it back and forth, like my mom used to do for me. His
frail body shivered under the thin checkered shirt's cloth. He
composed himself and stopped sobbing eventually, and then
told me he was from Seattle but his daughter was attending
school in D.C. When his wife died, his life ended. He was
completely lost without her. He retired a year ago and moved
to D.C. to be closer to his daughter. He was battling depression
and was willing to try just about anything to get his life moving again. He told me he tried dating twice, but both times he
felt so guilty about it. His wife was the love of his life and he
didn't want anyone else. I had no psychiatric background, and
being so young I had no experience with what he was going
through, but I knew he had had passion for this woman he had
shared his life with and I was touched. I know I probably
should've told him she'd want him to get on with his life and
all those other things you're supposed to say, but to this day I
know when I die I want someone to have loved me like that.

I didn't know what to tell him, so I asked him questions
about her, her likes and dislikes. I noticed a few antique cameras on display in a glass cabinet, and told him I was studying
photography. He was so happy to take the cameras out and
show me how they still worked. He pulled out photos of his
wife and daughter and I was sincere when I commented on how
beautiful they both were. Our time ran over and my pager
beeped. It was Miranda, calling to ask me if I was staying for
another hour, or what? If so, I'd have to charge him. I told him
I had to go and he happily paid the $100 for an extra half hour
with me. I couldn't believe this man was paying just for my

company. Thoreau was right. The mass of men *do* lead lives of quiet desperation.

He called the agency a few more times to see me, always ready with stories and sometimes lunch. We never did anything sexual or acted out fetishes or fantasies, and Miranda never knew he was any different from the "other freaks," as she called them. I ended up giving him my phone number and stopping by, for free, to check in on him from time to time. From every job I've ever had, no matter how miserable or insignificant, I've walked away with at least one true friend. Norman was it for this one.

A Recent Favorite

VIOLET BLUE

Mistress Natasha <MNatasha@therealblue.com> wrote:
> I'd like to hear your fantasy,
> about the first time we meet in
> person. Explain and elaborate for me, please.

> Suzanne Ramsey wrote:
A recent favorite:

I come over to your house for the first time. As we walk in, small talk is made, a little awkward smiling and laughing. You are seeing me for the first time; you like that I wore a skirt and blouse to meet you. I walk across your living room and make a point of checking out your couches. Light comes in through the window, revealing my legs, ass, and breasts through both skirt and blouse. I'm not wearing a bra.

Your telephone rings. You excuse yourself and answer. You're watching me look around the room as you talk. I wander over to the bookcase and pull out a title, thumbing through. It's important to you; you don't like people to be casual with that title. You put your hand over the phone and ask me to be careful. I look directly at you, and drop the book on the floor. It's loud. The person on the phone asks you what the noise was. You make a flustered excuse and hang up quickly. I am still looking at you.

Calmly, you walk over and ask me to pick up the book. I cross my arms and look out the window. You move very close to my face; you could kiss me if you wanted to. We have never kissed. I can smell your skin, your hair, your lipstick. I imagine that I can smell your anger. You can definitely smell my fear, but I do not move.

You slowly smile and reach behind me, snaking your hand up into my hair. It's soft. It feels good to me, your hot hand cradling my head. You squeeze your fist and get a handful of hair. I stiffen, unable to move. You move in closer, and your lips brush mine. You say, "Pick it up."

The light from the window on my face shows a veil of sweat beginning to cover my brow, nose, and upper lip. You step back and lower my head down toward the floor, toward the open book with its pages folded underneath it. I reach, and pick up the book. Bent over, you can see the rounded curve of my ass cheeks where they come together in the center. You bring me back up to standing. I look into your eyes, and I drop the book again.

More?

Mistress Natasha <MNatasha@therealblue.com> wrote:
> Definitely, more.

> Suzanne Ramsey wrote:
There is no sound. You look at the book, pages crushed again, then back to me. My breathing seems loud. A struggle of sound erupts in your apartment as you yank my head, leading me face-first by the back of the head toward the nearest couch. I wiggle and push away at your body, making little grunting noises and my feet scrape the floor. You've got my head fast and firm and I trip, falling onto my bare knees. You haul me back up, wailing now, dragging me on faulty legs. My knee is scraped, and my face is flushed red.

Jerking my head around, you sit on the couch. I am half-crouched, pitifully trying to stand. I can't see it, but your free hand finds its way to my blouse, my teacup breasts. A rough squeeze on one breast, then the other, and you pause to pinch and pull my nipple with your sharp, manicured nails. I give a little squeal. You pause, as if to appraise the noise, then move your hand to the center of my chest. With one rip, my blouse comes open. I gasp, and my eyes are wide as saucers.

I'm trying to move away, but I can't. This angers you further, and you haul me over your lap. Your businesslike pin-striped skirt roughly abrades my now-erect, pencil-eraser nipples. I struggle and kick in the air in futility. I can feel something hard through your skirt, poking me in the stomach.

You switch hands and press my face into the couch, where my sounds become muffled. With the other hand, my skirt gets hiked up over my bottom, with a little difficulty. I'm wearing sheer white panties, and the movement has settled them into

the crack of my ass. Suddenly I've become still. I'm frightened.
Shall I go on?

Mistress Natasha <MNatasha@therealblue.com> wrote:
> Nah, that's enough.
> Are you crazy? Of course go on! I order you.

> Suzanne Ramsey wrote:
I'm trying to be perfectly still, but you can feel me trembling a
little. My hips are moving slightly and you can feel them moving against the hardness between your thighs. The heat from
my pussy is radiating into your lap. You reach to cup a cheek in
your hand and I jump, startled at the soft touch. You grab a
handful of my ass and move it, so my panties go further into
my crack. My breathing is now labored, my mouth is open
against your couch. I can tell what the hardness is now—a
thick cock, strapped to your hips.

You grab the other cheek, and I start again. This annoys
you. I feel your hand move away, and you pull back and deliver
a hard smack, square on both cheeks. Crying out, I arch my
back and kick my feet into the couch like a petulant child. I'm
moving around on your lap, trying to somehow get away from
your monstrous hands. You grab the waistband of my panties
and lift me off your lap for a second; I hear a ripping sound.
You yank them off my hips, leaving angry red scrapes as I try
to make it more difficult for you. Your ever-erect cock is merci-
less, poking me every time I move.

The panties are shoved down around my knees and somewhat keep my legs together. I'm still wiggling, and you plant

another hard slap on my ass. The color is changing, and you can see two faint, almost abstract red hands emerging on my white skin. I'm gasping for air, and I arch my ass higher off your lap. It's as if I want more. You comply.

I moan when the third blow is landed, muffled and wet into the cushion. But you hit my ass harder the next time and I try to move away from you again. You pause and admire the color, rising and deepening. You pass your hand over it and feel that the skin is hot; I hiss from this sensation on my raw skin. You let go of my head and grab the back of my neck, still pressing me down, and deliver a series of sharp spanks, one after another as I yell, scream, and sob. I'm moving all over the place; I won't stay still.

You stop as I cry and take shortened breaths, but only to push the panties down more and shove one of my knees over your lap. My legs are spread now, and you have a full view of my ass and shaved pussy. It glistens. You put your whole hand, flat, over my vulva and cup my pussy. The wetness seems ridiculous, it's everywhere. You take two fingers and trace them over the puffy outer lips, drawing the wetness around. I'm finally quiet and still.

Your two fingers dip into the fold alongside my clit and you press; I stiffen. You slip your fingers down to my slit; it feels velvety. I relax. Your fingers slide inside me and I gasp. You leave them there. I wait. You do not move. I can't help it, I start to buck my hips toward your fingers, trying to fuck myself on your hand. You allow it for a moment; when I'm really losing myself you pull your hand away. I whine. You pull your hand back, and begin to spank my exposed pussy.

Had enough?

Mistress Natasha <MNatasha@therealblue.com> wrote:
  > Continue, if you please.

> Suzanne Ramsey wrote:
On the first blow, your hand hits my spread pussy with a wet smack. I jump and you have to grab my neck again, and though the spanks are lighter than the pummeling you gave my ass, I'm making mewling noises and breathing hard. On the third spank, my leg slides further to the floor, making my pussy wider. Next spank, you feel the soft, smooth wetness of my outer lips, and the bud of my swollen clit impacts your hand. You stop, push my body up so my pussy is centered above your lap, and reach to pull up your skirt.

I feel your hand under me as you unzip, move slightly, and your huge, hard cock presses against my pubic bone. The dildo is so warm; it is jet black and shiny like the glossy tresses you wear styled in a tight, prim updo. You move so the cock's fat head is between my outer lips and presses against my clit. With a slow, deliberate movement, you close my legs around your erection, engulfing it in the sticky wetness of my vulva and thighs. With my legs closed around it, you spank my ass, hard.

I scream and buck, inadvertently plunging your cock up and down the outside of my pussy. I can feel your heat, and I've gotten you all wet. You strike again, and when I writhe I keep my legs together, making a delicious suction around you. Again, and I howl, moving against you. Again, and I sob while your dildo rubs my clit in pleasure that's practically unbearable.

You realize you don't need to hold my neck down anymore. That's no fun for you. You roll me off of you, onto the floor. I look up at you on my knees, unable to sit down completely, so my legs are parted and my ass juts out obscenely. You tell me to come to you and lick you clean. You survey me: I'm red-faced, my makeup has made black rings under my eyes, my lipstick is smeared, my blouse is torn open, and my skirt is around my waist. You look perfect: a flushed yet stern librarian. My mistress. I move forward and begin to gingerly lick your sticky cock.

Are you still awake?

Mistress Natasha <MNatasha@therealblue.com> wrote:
> Although this is a very soothing and relaxing sort
> of bedtime story, I am, oddly,
> still awake. Continue, if you're up to it.

> Suzanne Ramsey wrote:
My little tongue flickers and grazes your cockhead. I jump when you bolt forward and grab my head with both hands. You put your face very close to mine. You inhale, and force a kiss on my mouth, deep and hard. Your tongue is unrelenting, and you crush my lips. You stop and say, "Like that."

I smile, and stick my tongue out at you. Forcing my head down, you press your cock on my lips, forcing them apart. I finally yield, and open my mouth around the huge object, sliding all the way down until the leather straps touch my nose. I choke and sputter. And suck.

You let go of my head and I start working your big black cock up and down in my mouth. I press my lips together to make a tight fit, and my cheeks go in slightly as I bob up and down. I'm enjoying it, showing off, devouring you. But I'm not supposed to like it too much, so you grab my hair again and pull me off, leaving my mouth in a shocked open "O" shape. You hold me still while your eyes burn a hole in me, while you stroke the dildo with the other hand, pulling and squeezing, pausing.

You let go and push me hard back onto my ass. I cry out from the pain and try to scuttle away to the side. I turn slightly to crawl but you're fast, on top of me, and I yell again from the rough fabric of your skirt on my very tender skin. On my stomach, I reach to claw the floor for traction but can't move. You've grabbed my hips with both hands and dragged me back to you, and I feel the big cock nose the opening of my pussy. In one tough thrust, you're in. And you stay there, still, while my pussy convulses around you.

You begin to move inside me, in short, hard thrusts. I'm breathing harder, balling my fists on the floor. You have my hips like handles, jerking me onto you, jerking you off into me. One hand releases and I feel your fingers press my clit, hard, and I start to buck on your cock, trying to make you go faster. You won't. I move harder, until I'm the one pushing into you. The pain of the skin on my ass is lost—until you let go of my clit, grab my hips again, and hold them down as you pull out. I begin to beg you to fuck me.

With both hands you grab my ass cheeks and I squeal. You part them and I know what is next. The slick, fat head of your cock pushes against the opening of my ass, nuzzling. Wetly, you begin to slide in, slowly at first; my breath is coming in heaves. Your head pops in; it's so tight in there, and I can feel my muscles spasming around the dildo. You pull my hips up off the floor, onto your cock, so you enter me all the way and I shriek. Leaning over, you reach in front of me to grab my breasts, and you roll my nipples between your fingers. I start to grind on your cock, and this time you oblige me, fucking my ass in a forced, jerky rhythm. Within a minute, my breathing has quieted. My nipples are very hard between your fingers; you know I'm about to come. You press farther inside me as the constriction becomes almost enough to push you out. You shove your fingers into my mouth, and at that instant, I exhale hard and you can tell my ass and pussy are squeezing down on your cock again and again as I rock back onto you, coming on your cock. You moan, and go over the edge of your orgasm. You explode and lose control. I feel you shudder and imagine your cum shooting into me, hot and wet.

Yours,
Suzanne

West 51st

THOMAS ROCHE

*S*o you like it, then? Anal sex," he said, his face reddening slightly as he asked the question over the remnants of dessert.

She looked at him over the rim of her glass, half of his face colored red with the wine, his eyes still blue through Waterford crystal.

"What kind of a question is that?" she said playfully, to cover the fact that she didn't know the answer.

It wasn't that she didn't know whether she liked anal sex—quite opposite. Truth be told, though she rarely told the truth, she preferred it to the "usual" kind, if anything could be called usual in San Francisco. She loved everything about it—that it was dirty, that it was taboo, that it made her a slut, and, not

least, that men wanted it so bad they would do just about anything for you once you'd let them fuck you in the ass—or, if
you played your cards right, to *get* you to let them fuck you in
the ass. She'd heard numerous female acquaintances talk about
how men always loved it and women always hated it. She felt
some obligation to educate those women, but it was an obligation she never, ever fulfilled. Her preference was a secret she
kept between herself and, well, every man she'd fucked since
college, actually.

She rarely came from vaginal intercourse unless there was a
vibrator involved. She *always* came from getting fucked in the
ass, no vibrator needed or wanted. She occasionally mused that
buried somewhere in her slutty little back door was a prostate
no one knew about except her and her lovers. She didn't seem
to have a G-spot, or if she had one it wouldn't come out to play,
so she figured God had accidentally given her a man's asshole,
which was fine with her since he'd kindly remembered to give
the rest of her ass a feminine shape.

But the thing she liked best about anal sex was something
that meant there was *no way*—not nohow, not nowhere—that
she was going to tell Bill the truth. Not for a little while yet, at
least.

"I'm sorry," he said, reaching across the destroyed tableau of
white chocolate petit fours to take her hand. "Maybe I'm being
too forward. I mean, we've only been together once."

Simone took a sip of her wine and smiled.

"It's not that," she said. "I just mean, it's not a real question. Do I like anal sex? Sure. I would love to fuck you in the
ass, Bill."

Bill stiffened, probably in more ways than one. Simone

could feel the tension in his hand that came from such a response. She could see his eyes all but spinning, cartoon style, in their sockets. Little cartoon birds might have been cavorting around his head.

Surely she would have told him the truth—that she loved being fucked in the ass, that the one time they'd been together she had been wishing the whole time he would go there, but had been too blissed out on the feel of him inside her to really care where he put it. Surely she would have told him, except that wasn't the kind of relationship they had.

Simone was a switch, sure, but she'd had a lot more experience as a submissive. It was only recently, upon a recent breakup, that she'd decided she wanted to try focusing on the other side of the mountain. She wasn't going to blow it all now with this new conquest, who liked to call her "mistress," who wanted to be spanked and have his balls tied, who liked to be called nasty things in bed and kiss her high-heeled shoes, who liked to be cuffed and forced to his knees and compelled with the threat of corporal punishment to go down on her until his salivary glands were swollen and red and he had to eat oatmeal for three days. She wasn't going to just let him flip her over and beg him to plow her back door, because said plowing always put Simone into the most deeply submissive space she ever experienced, turned her into a woman so insanely compliant and accommodating that she would do anything—*anything*—for the man whose cock she had in her ass.

Bill was a switch, too, that much was clear both from their conversations and from the long night together—well, actually, a night and morning, and most of an afternoon. But he'd answered her online ad headlined "30something professional woman wants to be your dominant bitch," not the online ad headlined "30something professional woman wants to be your submissive slut." Given that the dominant bitch had gotten thirty responses, fourteen of whom had turned out to be cross-dressers and eight of whom had been ex-boyfriends, whereas the submissive whore had gotten, at last count, one thousand four hundred eighty-seven responses, Simone wasn't going to flip that easily, even if she wanted to.

"Did I stop the conversation?" smiled Simone, caressing Bill's hand with hers. "Don't worry," she added, "I'm not going to force you. Well, all right, I *am* going to force you, but only because that turns me on. You'll have to sign off on it first."

"A notarized statement?" he said weakly, referencing an earlier conversation about the cops busting in while one of them was tied up.

"Consent to abuse, baby," Simone purred, an evil look on her face. "This is California. We'll get away with it."

"Don't I know it," said Bill.

"I don't think that's what you meant, was it?"

"About written statements?" said Bill nervously.

Simone cocked her head.

"Nooooo," she sighed. "About your earlier question. You're avoiding giving me a straight answer. Bill, that makes me very angry." She fixed his blue eyes with her brown ones, and licked her lips.

"You'd like me when I'm angry," she added.

Bill cleared his throat nervously. "I'm game," he said.

"But you haven't done it."

Bill shook his head quickly. She loved the way he got nervous when he admitted how inexperienced he was as a bottom.

"That is so sexy," she cooed. "I have a little virgin asshole to rape."

Bill's muscles tightened all over, probably in his ass, too. He always got so turned on when she used that word—it wasn't right for men to use it in that context, or at least polite men like Bill didn't use it outside the bedroom, and certainly not in forty-dollar-a-plate restaurants when discussing what was about to be done to their assholes.

"I love popping cherries," Simone sighed, rubbing it in. "Now I can't *wait* to get home. You did give me permission, remember? No changing your mind now."

It was part of their game, an amusement that had developed over the course of their last dinner together and the time they'd spent in bed. Both of them had the same kink: Once permission was given, reluctance was assured. Simone liked it that way. She was already wet.

"I'm having second thoughts," he said, and Simone could tell from the way he shifted in his seat that his cock was implacably, unyieldingly rigid, probably to the point where he couldn't stand up if he wanted to do it without social embarrassment.

"Good," said Simone. "You're buying dinner."

She finished off her wine and stood up, letting the waiter help her on with her coat. Technically it was her turn, the way such things usually went, but forcing Bill to break out his credit card gave her an extra little jolt of arousal, especially since he was about to become her bitch.

Or was she going to be *his* bitch? She'd never understood the use of that term. But then, for tonight at least, she didn't need to.

She left Bill there squirming with his hard-on while the waiter delivered the bill. Simone winked at Bill. "Don't keep me waiting," she said playfully, and walked toward the door.

The valet was cute, and Simone made a point of flirting with him as she handed him the ticket. If she could have, she would have brought the poor boy home with her to watch; that thought made her press her thighs together and try hard not to drip on the pavement.

Standing on the street smoking one of her rarely indulged in cigarettes, Simone felt the dizzy spin of arousal that made her a little bit worried she would pass out or maybe just fall down. Her cunt felt so swollen and tight that it hurt. Her clit throbbed with every thought that went through her mind. Her nipples were as hard as the pencil erasers everyone always mentions in those porn stories she wanked to from the Internet, and it wasn't because of the late-evening chill.

Did she dare tell him that, at least as far as this particular activity went, she was a virgin, too? I mean, sure, a finger or two during a particularly enthusiastic blow job, the occasional rim job that she always felt guilty about afterward and worried about parasites for six fucking months, but she'd never given a man a whole fucking dildo. She'd never even worn the fucking thing. She could only hope she hadn't thrown it away in her last flurry of spring cleaning.

No, she couldn't tell him. She was the top, she knew everything, right? Her job was to run the fuck like she knew what she was doing. Bill's job was to bend over and take it.

At least, she hoped that was the way it worked.

When Bill came out, she saw that he still had a lump in his

pants, and his face was red with humiliation. That didn't do anything to make her feel more steady; on the contrary, she thought she might shove him to his knees right there.

The valet pulled up in Simone's Jetta. "You're driving," she said to Bill. His eyebrows went up, but he opened the passenger-side door for her. Really, Simone just wasn't sure she *should* drive, not because of the three glasses of wine she'd had to Bill's two, but because she could barely focus her eyes, she was so fucking turned on. It felt deliciously dominant of her to make Bill be her chauffeur anyway.

He drove slowly, respecting the fact that this was Simone's car. That annoyed the living shit out of her, because all she wanted to do was to get the fuck home and fuck Bill's fucking brains out. She opened her mouth several times to say exactly that, more or less in those words, but she couldn't figure out how to say it without sounding totally out of control.

And control is what it was all about.

"Where to?" he asked as he pulled onto the main road. Right went to Simone's place on West 51st, left to Bill's in Tribeca.

"Right," she said.

"My bed is bigger," he said.

"But mine has all the strap-ons," she said.

Bill swallowed nervously.

"You're not really going to fuck me, are you?"

Simone sighed, laughed a little, and reached out to caress his face. Then she dropped her hand to his crotch and grabbed it, squeezing his cock as hard as she could.

Just then the light turned green, which was a good thing because Simone probably wouldn't have been able to stop herself from bending down and sucking Bill's cock, which would have spoiled everything.

"What do you think?" she asked him, and took her hand away. The car behind them honked.

It was a two-block walk from the garage where Simone parked her car to her one-bedroom apartment. She walked with her hand in Bill's back pocket, the way a particularly possessive metal-listening mullet-head might walk with his girlfriend.

Except that Simone's cock was bigger than any mullet-head's.

"You're sure you want to do this?" asked Bill as Simone handed him her house keys. On a "regular" date, it would have meant "Are you sure you want to sleep together? Really, it's okay if you don't. I like you as a person. We can just stay up all night and talk about the rainforest and French cinema. After all, it's only our second date."

But in this instance, it meant, and both of them knew it, "Are you sure you want to shove your cock into my ass?"

To which Simone responded with one hand grabbing Bill's cock and the other grabbing his ass—not one of his well-toned cheeks, but right in the middle, so her finger pushed firmly against his ass, right there under the klieg-light glare of West 51st Street.

"You'd better fucking believe I do," she said. "And I'm going to, no matter what you say, so shut the fuck up and get upstairs."

Bill's cock gave a spasm as she said that—she suspected more because of the words than because of her hand on his cock.

Simone was a potty mouth. She never ceased to amaze her lovers with the rank filth that could pour from her mouth in moments of passion. Except that usually it was "Fuck me in my fucking ass like I'm your fucking whore, Daddy," rather than "I fucking said get the fucking fuck upstairs you fucking little bitch, so I can fucking fuck your fucking tight virgin fucking ass, bitch," which is what she said, her body pressed up behind him and her lips against his ear, as Bill fumbled with the keys. In fact, she was rather impressed with herself, rarely being able to squeeze so many of her favorite word into one sentence. Maybe being a top *was* for her.

She punctuated her verbal filth with another firm grab of Bill's ass, which helped camouflage the fact that she needed to hold on to him to keep from falling down.

Bill finally found the right key and unlocked the three locks of Simone's apartment building. He stepped aside to let her enter first, which gave her a thrill—for an inexperienced bottom, he certainly knew how to be deferent. She gripped the railing and tried to make it look casual. She didn't feel drunk at all, but if she didn't get Bill into bed soon, she was going to fall down on the threadbare carpet and start twitching. She had never, ever been this turned on, certainly not after a second date.

She stepped aside and let Bill open her apartment door. He stepped aside and let her enter first.

As soon as the door was closed, she grabbed him and shoved him against it, planting her mouth on his. If she hadn't been wearing three-inch heels, she wouldn't have even be able to reach him. His cock, however, would have been right at mouth height if she had dropped to her knees. But fuck that, those were her old habits. Tonight, Bill was going to be the one sucking.

"Get your clothes off," she said, pointing at the tiny bath-room. Bill scampered in there and closed the door behind him.

"And no stalling!" she said as she raced for the bedroom.

In fact, Simone hoped that Bill *would* stall, because not only did she have to get undressed, but she had no fucking idea how the strap-on worked. She had never worn it herself; it was a remnant of a bi fling she'd had five years ago, one of those things an ex forgets at your place when she or he leaves for the last time, like his Harry Connick Jr. albums or her ancient, faded "I Got a Blow Job on Bourbon Street" T-shirt.

Simone stripped off her clothes in record time, kicking off her shoes, stuffing the coat, the blouse, the skirt, and the bra into the black of the closet—she'd cleaned for six hours on the off chance that they'd come here instead of going to Bill's place, and she wasn't going to start throwing clothes around now.

She muttered one of her potty-words when she realized that she'd put her panties on over her garters. *Should I wear my garter belt with a strap-on?* she thought. No time to worry about it. She unhitched the garters, stripped off the belt, and left the black seamed stockings. Thank God they were stay-ups.

Between digging under her old blankets and looking under the bed, she decided she should put the shoes back on. They gave her kind of a femme-fatale look, and besides, if she found herself standing up the *last* thing she wanted was to be a whole foot taller than her little ass-bitch, as she'd begun to affection-ately think of him.

She finally found the strap-on and its accompanying dildo on the third shelf of her closet, stuffed into a hat box full of dime-store porn. She was pretty sure she had washed it the last time she had used it, but giving it a quick rinse was out of the question—Bill was still in the bathroom.

Luckily, her little ass-bitch was, in fact, stalling. That gave her the five minutes or so she needed to figure out the leather straps of the harness and force the frustratingly large dildo through the too-tight ring. When she looked at herself in the full-length mirror next to her bed, she made a confused face, *Was it supposed to fucking hang like that?*

She heard the bathroom door opening and went to hop onto the bed, at the last moment remembering to dim the lights. The soft feel of faux leopard fur caressed her bare ass as she sank into the cheap mattress. She tried hard to affect a casual-looking posture, like she'd been relaxing there for hours waiting for some fine stud, preferably a lawyer, to come by and polish her knob.

She was out of breath, though, and couldn't have looked casual if her life depended on it. Luckily, Bill didn't barge in but knocked tentatively at the door. Simone had closed it when she was ransacking her room for the harness.

"Wait," she said, taking a perverse pleasure at making him relax while she took deep breaths and tried to relax.

"Yes, Mistress" came Bill's small voice from the other side of the door.

"All right," she said when she felt as properly situated as she was likely to get. "Come in, ass-bitch."

Bill opened the door. All the frenzied searching and strap-buckling of the last few minutes vanished as Simone looked him up and down. He was naked, his cock still hard as a rock, pointing toward the ceiling much more than her dildo would have been if it hadn't been lying against her belly.

What's more, Bill's eyes went wide as he saw the dildo, the size of it plainly troubling him.

"What?" Simone smiled, her voice suddenly playful. "You beg me to fuck you and now you're going to complain about how big my cock is? Come now, Bill, if a girl tried to pull that, do you know what her boyfriend would do?"

She didn't even have to say the word—it was so politically incorrect for him to even think it, for her to imply it, that it gave an immediate boost to his cock. She could see it spasming slightly all the way across the room.

"Come over here," she said. "And show me what a little bitch like you does to a nice big cock like this."

Bill closed the bedroom door behind him—a good thing, because the walls here were paper thin and Simone fully intended to make a whole fucking lot of noise. Bill took tentative steps to the bed, his cock rising and falling slightly with the beat of his heart.

"Come on," Simone said, teasingly cocking her finger. "Come hither, bitch. Show me what you do with a big fat cock."

Bill clearly did not know what one did with a big fat cock. As he climbed onto the bed, Simone took him in her arms, and he gingerly wrapped his hand around it, like he was handling a dead rat.

"No," she said patiently. "That's not what a little fucking slut whore like you wants to do with a big fat fucking cock, is it, bitch?" She smiled sweetly, seeing the effect of her words in Bill's eyes. Something hungry pulsed in them, but it was when she took hold of his head and pushed him down to her crotch that she knew she'd found the right button.

Bill took the head of Simone's cock into his mouth and began sucking it. Simone uttered a long, satisfied moan as she watched his mouth go gliding up and down on it. He could only take a third of it into his mouth, but the sight of him struggling to take more excited Simone enough to make her grab his hands and plant them on her breasts. He obediently pinched and rubbed her nipples as his head bobbed up and down in her lap.

"Deeper," she said, and felt a wave of excitement building as he struggled with the head pushing against the back of his throat.

"Deeper," she moaned softly, feeling the shudder of Bill's body as he gagged. She loved that feeling herself, of being compelled to take cock as deep as it would go in her throat—so deep she gagged, so deep she choked. The last thing she wanted to do was choke Bill. But making him cry a little bit was still on the menu.

And as Bill struggled with his gag reflex, she achieved just that. Simone's clit throbbed against the base of the dildo when she saw Bill's eyes grow moist with gag-induced tears. She breathed hard and pushed his hands more firmly against her tits, encouraging him to pinch harder. But when the first tear leaked out of his eye and ran down his cheek, dribbling warm and succulent onto Simone's belly, she couldn't wait anymore.

She grabbed Bill's hair and pulled him off her cock. Smiling, she kissed him.

"Ready to become my little whore?" she purred.

"No," said Bill nervously, but the flash in his eyes told Simone everything she needed to know—that, and the fact that he had not yet said "rutabaga," or even "marching band."

She grabbed his arm and threw him bodily onto the bed, facedown—something that would have been damn well impossible if Bill hadn't been under her spell.

Simone knelt behind Bill on the full-size bed, running her hands up the backs of his thighs. "Lift your ass," she growled. "Up on your knees, bitch. Face on the pillow."

She realized after she said them that she had heard those exact same words from more than one lover with her in Bill's position. What the hell? They worked.

Parting Bill's cheeks with her thumbs, she saw the tight pink hole she was about to ravage. The sight of it made her hungry.

"Get me the lube," she told him. "It's in the nightstand."

The "nightstand" was actually a plastic office caddy, but Bill got the idea. He found the tube of thick lubricant, his hands shaking as he nervously handed it down to Simone.

A thick dollop of lube made him gasp with the coldness as she caressed his asshole with her thumb. She stroked him in small circles as she felt him relaxing, the tension going out of his ass as he gave himself up to what was about to happen.

She slipped first one finger—her middle—then two— middle and index—into Bill's ass. He grunted and pushed back against her. She added more lube and fucked him some more. Bill shivered and ground his hips against the bed. "Up!" she snapped. "Up on your knees. Face in the pillow. Hands at your sides."

Bill obeyed; Simone adored this position. It made one look so small and vulnerable. Of course, it was usually her in this position, but that only turned her on more. She growled "Higher!" and Bill obediently raised his ass as far as he could while Simone's lubed fingers slid deeper into his ass, taking their time, opening him up. She added a third finger, with just a tad more lube, and Bill began to gasp obscenities.

She spanked him again, never taking her other hand out of his ass. "I'll tell you when to curse, bitch!" she barked. "I'll tell you when to fucking curse, and right now all you do is fucking moan and fucking whimper, you got that?"

Bill nodded, complying with both instructions as he wriggled and pushed against Simone's hand, his hips working rhythmically. She got all three fingers in deeper, adding lube. The feel of his ass, tight and virgin around her fingers, had her so wet she could feel the moisture dripping down her thighs.

As she fingered his ass, Simone reached between his legs and felt his cock. Still hard—if anything, harder than ever. He moaned as she stroked his cock.

"You like that, bitch?" she purred. "You like having your fucking ass plowed while I fuckin' jerk your cock, bitch?"

"No," he moaned softly. "Please . . . please don't."

She spanked him on the ass, hard.

"I'll tell you when to beg!" she snapped. "Just for that you're not getting any more lube! You're going to take my cock dry!"

"Yes, Mistress," whimpered Bill pathetically.

Of course, Simone had already added a healthy dollop to the head of her cock, smearing it around so the implement glistened in the dimmed lights. But the threat was worth it; Bill squirmed and whimpered with arousal as Simone gripped his cock harder.

She withdrew her three fingers from his asshole and wiped them on his back. Her cunt pulsing with arousal, Simone nestled up behind Bill and snapped at him to spread his legs wider. He did, straining to lift his ass as high as he could

"Now, this is going to hurt you more than it does me," she said breathlessly, fitting the thick head of her cock into the notch of Bill's ass.

But in fact, when she pushed it in, it didn't seem to hurt, which was the whole point. She could tell. The moans he gave were not the real-pain moans when she'd tweaked his nipples or spanked him hard last weekend, but the faked-pain moans when she'd suckled on his nipples or spanked him softly.

That only made her shove her cock into his asshole harder, burying the thick member deep inside Bill.

"Oh, fuck," gasped Bill, his back straightening as he was forcibly filled up.

Simone slapped his ass hard. "What did I tell you?" she snarled. "Did I tell you to curse?"

Bill shook his head emphatically, and went back to moaning and whimpering, exactly what she'd told him to do.

But he also pushed himself back onto her cock, his cheeks spreading around the thick shaft as he ground against her.

Simone began fucking him. It was a difficult matter at first, requiring her to get on one knee and one foot, driving into him at a cockeyed angle. But she got the hang of it within a dozen thrusts. Bill groaned as she started fucking him harder.

She reached under him and found his cock hard. "You want to touch it? You want to fucking jerk off while I fuck you? Answer me, bitch! I asked you a direct question!"

"Yes, Mistress," he grunted. "Please let me jerk off."

"No!" she shrieked. "Not until I'm good and ready!" She was so turned on that she had to hold his hips to steady herself.

That gave her the perfect handhold to slam him back onto her cock, making him groan each time the thick head reached its deepest point inside him.

Simone's head spun. God, she wanted her little ass-bitch to come. She wanted to let him jerk off while she fucked him, but she should really come first, shouldn't she? After all, she was in charge, wasn't she?

"What are you?" she snapped, finally deciding she couldn't wait another minute to see Bill twisting and writhing in orgasm.

"What?" he moaned softly.

She spanked his ass rapidly as she fucked him, matching the rhythm of her cock going into him with hard blows to his ass. "I—said—what—the—fuck—are—you?"

She wasn't going to just hand it to him—not now, not when he was so ready to come.

"I . . . I . . ."

"Say it! Tell me what you are!"

She almost uttered the words "Are you my little ass-bitch?" But she managed to stop herself at the last moment, because Bill blurted it out.

"I'm your little fucking ass-bitch," he groaned.

Simone liked the idea of saying it so much that she couldn't stop herself. She growled: "Say it with me."

"Mistress, I," she began.

"Mistress, I," Bill matched her.

"I am," she said, louder.

"I am your . . ." he began.

"I am your little fucking . . ."

They both said the whole sentence together. "I am your little fucking ass-bitch," and Simone leaned as far forward as she could, grabbing Bill's wrist and shoving his hand down between his legs.

Then she started to fuck him again, harder than ever, as she said, "Show me how much it fucking turns you on to be my little ass-bitch!"

"Yes, Mistress," he groaned, wrapping his hand around his cock. Simone's head spun as she felt his body bucking against her—it was ten seconds, maybe, no more, before he lifted his head, threw it back, spasmed all over like nothing Simone had ever seen.

He shot his load all over Simone's faux leopard bedspread. She plowed him as deep as her cock would go, shoving the toy to its deepest point inside him while Bill's orgasm tore through him.

She had never experienced it before—the way his asshole tightened and jerked around her cock as he came, sending unbelievable sensations into her body. God, she fucking had to come.

She managed to wait until he finished coming before she drew her cock out of him—slowly, forcing herself to go slowly, with overwhelming, intense difficulty—and shoved him forward with a firm hand on his lube-smeared ass.

The harness came off easier than it had gone on. Maybe it was because she just got one leg undone and then yanked the thing down her other leg, throwing it vaguely toward the closet as she crawled up the bed and spread her legs.

"Fucking do me, you little fucking bitch," she said. She thought Bill would be dull and listless after his orgasm, but his face went right between her spread legs, right where it belonged, with a swiftness that excited her. His tongue worked its way between her lips, molding to her clit. He began to service her as she twisted her fingers in his hair—it was a little too short to properly pull, but she had to do *something* with her hands.

Bill did something with his hands, too, without being told—he reached up to Simone's breasts and firmly pinched her nipples, the way she liked.

"Fuck yeah, eat me out, you fucking ass-bitch," Simone was about to say, but it just blurred together into one long weird expletive that, had an outsider heard it, would have seemed like a mix of Russian, Turkish, and caveman-speak. Her ass came up off the bed and Bill's mouth rode her cunt flawlessly, his tongue working her clit as she cursed and thrashed in orgasm. Her thighs worked back and forth violently, so much so that halfway through, she was afraid she had boxed his ears.

But when she finally finished and relaxed into the bed, Bill heard her perfectly when she moaned, "Get up here."

She might have been afraid that the way she put her arms around his big chest, the way she snuggled into his flesh and drew a deep breath to smell him, the way she curled into a ball in his arms—it was all so fucking *submissive*. In that white-hot instant of her orgasm, she had gone from a thirty-something professional woman who wanted to be his dominant bitch to, well, to whatever. She didn't care, about that or about the leopard-print bedspread that Bill had soiled with his cum and now with his lube-smeared ass. She didn't care about much, except the smell of his body and the feel of it against her.

Bill held her as she shuddered all over, her cunt still spasming from her orgasm.

"I'm your little ass-bitch," he said softly, with a weird kind of smile in his voice.

She didn't even look up to see if Bill was smiling for real.

"Yeah," Simone breathed. "You're telling me."

Transfixed, Helpless, and Out of Control: Election Night 2004

CHARLIE ANDERS

*Q*ueerdom cries. The hot young things at Eighteenth and Castro gather around the world's suckiest television screen, made out of bedsheets and milk crates, watching the world turn red. "It's okay," people keep saying over and over again, "Ohio's still a toss-up." Over in the Midnight Sun, it's almost a relief when they show a Village People video instead of Dan Rather's folksy ramblings. Dan Rather says the election is as sticky as a squirrel in heat covered with forest burrs. He says John Kerry is as desperate as a nudist in a freak hailstorm.

Queer theory didn't prepare you for this, did it? The solidity of the PatriArchy Bunker, the flubbery resilience of the warlike phallus. Everywhere I look, tragedy strikes down Gay

Shame and the Marriage Equality people alike. Even the Village People are not enough to rescue our crumbling psyches. Skinny fags and dykes in tight shirts and pants look as though someone just set fire to their gourmet dog-biscuit store.

"But, but . . . I mean, Kerry won Maryland," this one girl says through tears and hair and maybe snot. She's normally kempt, but the election returns are challenging her kemptness. We're looking at the screens on the outside of the Midnight Sun, on the sidewalk. "That's good, isn't it? Maryland's in the South, sort of. He won a southern state." Seeing her so desperate, so miserable, so, so . . . achy for a promised reward, suddenly I'm all horny. She has that look, the one that bottoms get when you've promised them an orgasm if they'll just do one little thing for you, and then it turns out you lied.

I like that look. I go to great lengths to elicit it from my bottoms.

I will now cut and paste a paragraph from my last Craigslist ad, to avoid having to describe myself in this story. "I'm forty-two years old, but can pass for forty-one. Been an SM dyke since the Iran-Contra scandal. Mostly bony but with some curves. Brown hair, brown eyes, fair skin. Leather-wearing femme. Sadistic and sarcastic, but not Socratic." There, now you've got a mental picture. Bully for you.

Before I've consciously thought about it, I've decided unkempt girl is my prey. She has latte-colored skin and long wavy hair. Turns out her name is Lexa and she's an MFA student at State. She's still crying over John-boy and his terrible shortfall. NBC has called Ohio for Bush, but everyone else is reserving judgment.

It's not looking good, is it? I ask her, not having to fake my own disappointment. It feels so useless to be standing around here, watching and waiting . . . I sigh theatrically.

"Yes, I feel so awful," Lexa says. "And yet, transfixed."

The way she says the word "transfixed" gets me all hot again. Don't ask me why, it just does. I want to transfix her.

Like a train wreck, I say. You want to look away, but you can't.

"Exactly," she says. "Helpless."

I have to bite my lip when she says that word. I sigh again, ostensibly at the election results. Yes, I say. But at times like this, it's good just to be close to another human. To feel alive. Do you know what I mean?

She says she does, but I know she doesn't. I chat with her some more: about the stupidity of the electoral college, all those huge empty red states where nobody lives deciding who gets to be president, the gerrymandering of the House of Representatives, the corporate ownership of the media, does democracy even exist anymore? Blah blah blah. Paralysis seeps into her limbs, like bondage without any torture except for the slow death of hope.

I feel the need to rescue her from all this, to replace her mental anguish with another type of pain.

Don't get me wrong, I'm upset, too. The thought of four more years of Bush, of Bush with a mandate between his mandibles, fills me with creeping sickness. It's not just her I'm trying to rescue. My lust is a welcome distraction.

I whisper in her ear, caress with words: It's late, there's nothing we can do here, they won't call the election tonight, there's still hope, it seems silly to let the night end with anticlimax, why don't you come back to my place for some tea and cakes, we can keep an eye on the results from there. . . . She nods, slowly.

I live in Outer Noe Valley, past Lovejoy's Tea House. Tea and cakes are very important to me. They symbolize politeness, friendliness, companionship, stickiness—all good things. My apartment is sort of a Steampunk railway car, with a small dungeon area next to the computer, which looks piston-powered but isn't.

While Lexa is looking around with what I hope is a mixture of terror and admiration for my decor, I busy myself with scones and decaf Earl Grey. Clotted cream, strawberry jam. We must keep up our strength, I purr. Lexa is staring at the small but impressive bondage area: rings in the ceiling and floor, sling pinned up on one wall, an assortment of floggers and torture devices on a lacquer tray. The whole thing soundproofed with big tapestries, including one a friend gave me that shows the traditional unicorn getting ass-fucked by the virgin with a strap-on.

I make loud tea-serving noises behind her so she won't feel as though I'm sneaking up on her. I hand her a cup and saucer, gesture to the milk and sugar in their floral china homes. I touch her wrist and she nearly spills. This could be our last chance, I say. To enjoy life. Before the repression starts.

"Oh no," she says. "There's still hope. Maryland, I mean. And Ohio is a toss-up!"

Yes, yes. Always hope. And meanwhile, I offer her a scone, but she's not hungry. I ask her if she likes my bondage gear, and she says yes. Sometimes, I say, transgressive sex can be an act of resistance against hegemony. She likes that, as I knew she would.

WHIPPED

I put my hand on the back of her neck and she moans. Just a light touch. She's still holding the teacup, which keeps her from making any sudden movements. I run my fingers down her neck and along her shoulder, through her sweater. I finally take the tea away from her and put it down on the little table next to my computer. I come back to her, she hasn't moved, and I run my fingers over her cheek. She closes her eyes, goes into a mild trance. I keep stroking her cheek, run my other hand over her body without touching it. She can just feel my palm pass by her breasts, stomach, cunt, without touching.

I tell her to take off her sweater. It's an over-the-head thing that leaves her blinking and muss-haired. I stroke her lips with my finger and she opens her mouth to take it inside. I undo the clasp of her jeans with the other hand.

This could be our last night of freedom, I tell her. We have to be prepared for the worst. She's given up on contradicting me. Her jeans fall to the floor, bunched around her boots. Now all she's wearing is an antiglobalization T-shirt, panties, and boots. I tell her to shout "red state" if I do anything she doesn't like. She nods.

I tell her to undo her boots and mine, to save time and to maximize the time she spends bent over. Her ass is even more amazing in panties than it was in jeans. It would make an excellent center of resistance, it could contain the revolution in its roundness. When she stands up again, I stroke her thighs with almost no pressure at all. She's a fun bottom, she twitches just from a little petting. Skittish.

You're lucky, I tell her. A pretty one. They'll keep you to breed the next generation of Jesus droolers. You'll learn to like reading the (and here I smack her left butt cheek) Left Behind books. You'll be a good fundy wife, in time.

She pushes her ass back to meet the spanking halfway. I swat too lightly to hurt, until she begs me to spank her harder. I pull her panties off, leaving her wearing just the T-shirt. I move her panties, jeans, socks, and boots out of the way, then guide her ankles to the rings in the walls of my little bondage cubbyhole. I put Velcro cuffs around her ankles and snap them onto the rings. I leave her arms free, so she could free her ankles in seconds. But I know she won't, and this way her legs are spread nicely. I make her bend over slightly so I have a nice view of her ass and pussy.

Now that I'm sure she's not going to run away, I can commence the mind-fuck in earnest. Oh, I mean it's not really a mind-fuck, it's catharsis, it's helping her to confront the inevitable. Not really mind-fuck at all.

I spank her harder and tell her all the horrible things that will happen. Polluters will rewrite all the environmental regulations and pollute our wetlands. (Here I brush her own wetlands, just a little.) The FBI will place us all under surveillance in the name of Homeland Security. (Whap!) Antonin Scalia will be chief justice. (I claw her back under her T-shirt.) Abortion rights will wither. (Smack!)

I get my suede flogger and start on her ass and thighs. Perversely, I don't want to take off her T-shirt yet. You thought things were going to change? I say, giving her nice even strokes back and forth, mixed with little cooling touches. Well, they'll change, all right—you're going to learn what patriarchy's all about! Are you excited?

"No," she sobs. She's biting her lip to keep from crying. It's delicious, for a moment it's almost worth another four years of Dubya. Almost. "No, I hate it."

I know, it's scary, I say. Do you want to feel nice for a while, to take your mind off it?

She nods and blinks. Now I pull her T-shirt up, but not all the way off. I leave it covering her head, so her arms are raised and she's blindfolded. I tell her not to move it. Then I start stroking her breasts, her sides, her armpits. Some of my touches make her purr and twist her body, others make her jump a little from ticklishness. She's lost in sensation.

Then I start in again, predicting. A few rich CEOs will control the entire economy, you'll be their slave. Your vegan boutiques will turn into Gap outlets. We'll turn the whole Middle East into a crater.

And so on. The whole time I'm giving her little touches, licks, and bites on her thighs, breasts, stomach. She's torn between panic at the horrors I'm spinning out and the messages her skin is sending her. I put a latex glove on one hand and lube up a finger. I smear lube around her ass and she moans louder, rotating her butt in supplication. I keep fingering and whispering in her T-shirt-covered ear.

They'll teach creationism in school, I murmur. They'll ban sex education and teach everyone that masturbation causes AIDS. My finger is pressing against her butthole now, just a friendly introduction. She pushes back. Pretty soon my finger is moving in and out and around, slicking her inside and out. She's bucking and gasping. They're going to round up the queers and put us in camps, I say. She wails.

I'm just getting warmed up. I keep finger-fucking her ass

with my left hand and flogging her shoulder blades with my right hand. I can't flog too hard, because it's hard to coordinate and I don't want the flogger to wrap around accidentally. But it still stings. Pleasure below, pain above.

We're this close to a military dictatorship, I say, snapping the flogger against her shoulder blades. She squeals. All it takes is one little shove . . . I push my finger farther into her ass . . . and we'll turn into real fascists. I work a second finger into her ass and she once again backs up to welcome it in. They'll suspend the Constitution and the Bill of Rights. I'm not even trying to be gentle anymore, the fingers are thrusting and the T-shirted head and arms are flailing. The feds will strip-search you in the streets, whenever they feel like it. They'll cavity-search you.

Somewhere inside the antiglobalization shirt a little voice is begging, "No, no, no, no . . ."

I decide to check in. Are you doing okay? Are you ready to cry "red state" yet?

"I'm okay," she says between sobs. "Please don't stop."

That's all I needed to hear. Are you ready to be cavity searched by Homeland Security? She cries and says "No" over and over again. I keep claiming her ass. Are you ready for Christian reeducation camps?

"No, no, no, no, no!"

I get a butt plug and ease it into the opening I've made. I let her know that if she lets it fall out, I will leave her tied up and tell Tom DeLay where to find her. She whimpers like a puppy. The butt plug stays in. Good girl. I take off the glove.

I whip her tits, then finger her pussy, then whip her tits some more. I put a couple of Day-Glo clamps on her nipples and then whip her tits again, flicking them back and forth.

In the new world, women will be property, I hiss in her ear. You'll have to act like Laura Bush, stand behind your man.

My fingers circle around her clit. It trembles. Oh yes, you'll enjoy being Hester in our Puritan new world. I get a Hello Kitty vibrator and work her clit with it. I move closer to her clit every time I say something to upset her.

Bzzzz . . . Hate crimes will become public policy. "Oh yes, please yes!" Bible study will be mandatory. "Please, yes, please don't stop!" We'll all have to swear loyalty to Bush. "Yes, yes, yes!" They'll have a curfew at night and all day Sunday except for church. "Oh God, more!"

Finally, just as I'm telling her that Congress will mandate public burnings of queer books, she screams as if it's her last breath, she shakes and flails and the butt plug flies out of her and she goes rigid and then collapses.

Ankles still cuffed, she leans against one wall, her body slack. Reality seeps back into her mind. All the things I said before unspool again, only this time without the thrill of bondage and arousal to soften them. She's left mostly naked, really helpless, in a terrifyingly ugly world.

I ask her if she'd like to come back sometime soon, and she says yes.

From the Private Diary of Mistress Ilsa

ILSA STRIX

February 1, 2001: G.I. Joe in Heels

The past two months have been an absolute whirlwind of activity, starting with Hawaii in early December, then a couple of days in Laguna Beach, a few days in San Francisco to celebrate New Year's, a few days in Las Vegas, a few more days in Laguna Beach, a week in San Francisco, and finally a weekend at a spa in Mexico. To top this off I have had a stunning time in my dungeon, taking very few scenes but making sure they are as pure and powerful as possible.

Take today, for instance, with my dear slave whom I will refer to as G.I. Joe, for that is exactly what he looks like, from the top of his stubble-shaved head to his solid, carved jaw to the thick meatiness of his overworked pectorals to his "run fifty miles in a week," "squat with five hundred pounds" thighs. His air is military as well, all business with that deadpan seriousness in his dark eyes that shades a little-boy awe when I walk into the room.

I haven't seen him in a few months, giving me time to think about how good he looks when he is doing my bidding, making me look forward to these hours I get to put him through the paces.

Joe is all brawn and meaty manliness, cut from the legacy of the military elite. He knows how to follow orders and enjoys when I really lay into him, whether that be with commands, humiliation, or actual physical pain; the more I get into his head, the better he feels. There is a certain type of military man, generally Special Forces (Navy SEAL, Marine, etc.), who really understands, on a base level, the give and take of power. They seem preprogrammed to react well to harsh environments as they actually enjoy the challenge. A large number of my favorite slaves have been soldiers, and without fail they like it hard and heavy, taking it like a man, relishing how severe I can go.

One of the things I like best about Joe is how great he looks in a pair of six-inch pumps. The juxtaposition is enough to accommodate the complexity of my psychosexual landscape as I bind his substantial arms behind his back so his rippling chest protrudes even more, lock him into heavy chains, and tether his feet so he must walk in tiny, dainty steps. G.I. Joe in stilettos, his balls locked into a leash system so I can make him walk, trot, canter, and, without his chains, gallop at my whim.

I am in the mood for a bit of equine play. Tuesday afternoon

I went riding in Simi Valley. My horse and I were in fine spirits, my spurs giving him the right persuasion as we cantered across the desert floor and up into dry windswept mountains. I have been riding Jesse, a chocolate brown steed with a white lightning stripe, for several months now, and our rides get better and better as I learn how to properly motivate him. I find that by angling my toes and gripping him tightly between my thighs, he will stay at a perfect gait, allowing me the most enjoyment for my ride. But I digress. After putting Joe through a series of physically intensive dressage exercises, enough that a glistening of sweat appeared over his chiseled lips, I proceeded to immobilize him in the sit sling, connecting his silver high heels to his beefy derriere, his arms pinned together behind his back, his burly lats pushing into the heavy well-oiled leather, his eyes half shut in dreamy anticipation. I stick a Nat Sherman "queen size" cigarette into the holder, light it, and then while exhaling proceed to take him on a verbal journey.

"Take my smoke, inhale me. You are going take me today—be good for me—be your very best for me." I am leaning over him, my leather-gloved hand firmly holding the back of his shorn head, whispering in his ear, my corseted breasts just inches from his face. "You did well today but you are a bit out of shape—only ran fifty miles this week? Next week run seventy-five. Only bench-pressed three twenty-five? Get it up to three fifty. I don't want to see you slack, don't want to see you get sloppy on me." I blow a thin stream of smoke in his face.

"I am planning on showing you off, taking you on a little outing, and for this you need to be perfect, both physically and mentally. I want all of your steps precise; each time that stiletto hits the floor I want your toe to come down first, then your heel, graceful. I want your shoulders back as far as they can go, your stomach in—speaking of which," as my leather-covered finger traces the rippled indentations of his abdomen, "perhaps you should think about cutting down on some of those carbs. I want you cut when I finally decide to take you out, not an ounce of extra, just pure clean lines and heaps of well-defined muscle." More smoke in his face, this time he coughs a bit.

"Ahem. You need to learn to take my smoke, allow those pure, well-exercised lungs to absorb me, take me in. Think of it as a wolf marking her turf. You will need to be able to inhale seamlessly, as the equestrian center that I am taking you to has a smoking area on the north side where all the ladies sit in their heels and watch as the pony boys and girls are trained. If you do poorly—that is, if you stumble, have poor posture, or react slowly—they will undoubtedly want to see you punished, and, of course, so will I, as it will be a poor reflection of these years we have spent fine-tuning you. If you do well, making me proud, then you will be rewarded. Both reward and punishment might include smoke torture and high-heel worship, but the tone will be different—extremely different." A stream of smoke to his eyes, but he struggles to keep them open despite the oncoming tears.

My short, ruffled petticoat jumps, and I realize how excited the slave is getting. I move back to see better. "It is amazing how evident you men are, doesn't it make you just a bit ashamed, a bit embarrassed when you are aroused by such depravity? When you cannot conceal your excitement? When it is there, in plain sight for all to see, all to comment about and possibly laugh at?" I grab his testicle leash, pulling the chain roughly toward me. The sit sling moves and he is hanging, partially suspended by his genitals. "Imagine that you get this aroused in front of the dozen or so smoking, high-heeled women who will be watching your debacle. How will it feel to know that not only are they watching your humiliation, but they also see what a fiercely wound-up creature it makes you? However will you rationalize that level of humiliation?" I move my face closer, forcing his down-turned eyes to watch my heavily rouged lips as they inhale the smoke, as my tongue moistens them, and then as they exhale, slowly. He opens his mouth and his body goes rigid, every muscle pumped, flexed. He inhales my smoke as if it is his last breath. The muscles in his neck are twitching and I am enjoying how I can control the beast; there is a thrill in taming him, torturing him, winding him up, and tying him down. He strains against the leather, making the leash pull harder on his groin, making him all that much more aroused, making his torment that much greater.

I lean in ever closer, wanting him to smell my hair, to know acutely what he can't have. I then bring the leash between his legs and walk around to his back, pressing up against him, the stiff leather of my corset against the hardness of his back, pulling his balls up and under him. I hear his sharp intake of breath as my hand wrenches the chain backward across the deep cleft of his ass; in doing so his upper body is pulled forward, downward, so that any movement at all will result in searing pain.

I know I have him just where I want him.

February 27, 2001: Valentine

He arrives early, thinking that this is the best solution, rather than be late.

Roxy lets him in, commenting that Ilsa will be arriving at the appointed time, that promptness is key. Ahem.

He sits with a cool, calculating piece of paper that he was instructed to fill out, on one side a legal disclaimer, signing away his rights, on the other, a checklist of his desires. Staring at the form, he ponders its metallic air, how dissociated this is from the intimacy of power and trust. How can I, he thinks, know what urges dwell within, when I have not yet met her, when I know not what desires she arouses. How impersonal, this checklist, like a bare-bones menu of perversions, no adjectives, no flavor, just the hard cutting reality of actions aloof from interaction.

He imagines what she will bring out in him, but it is to no avail, he has so little experience, so little knowledge of what the words mean other than as removed concepts. He checks off what is possibly tolerable, unsure as to how much to reveal, unsure of how much trust to put on paper.

The game is beginning already, with a piece of paper she has put him off balance, such simple torment, leaving him helpless to face his desires, without him even having seen her.

The minutes tick endlessly by, punishment for his early arrival, he is left with the paper, his needs, and his apprehensions. Their brief telephone call, a hurried confirmation, left him with more questions than answers.

For a moment he considered getting up and leaving, to end the torment, but already something held him captive in her dungeon. Perhaps it was knowing that leaving would only increase his distress, or perhaps it was that those cold impersonal words reeked of experiences to be had, or perhaps, just perhaps, it was that he had a small inkling of the endless possibilities of this moment in time.

She was in the dressing room, applying a first coat of lipstick, blotting it, powdering it, then applying a second thick red layer, finally coating it all in a slick gloss of clear lacquer, her lips now multidimensional, a polished crimson world unto themselves. A slight annoyance at her subject's premature arrival showed in the corners of her mouth.

Roxy saw this and tried to compensate. "He seemed really nice," she offered weakly. "I think you'll like him, he has cute earrings."

She wasn't impressed, hated being rushed, but tried to push the displeasure out of her mind, slowly applying a final coat of mascara, attending to each individual lash, leaning so close to the mirror that a small steam rose across the surface of the glass.

Sometimes a bit of irritation worked to her advantage, taking the agitated energy and allowing it to heat the scenario, allowing it to give the needed edge.

She stood back and admired her work, straightening her corset, taking in her reflection with pleasure. She glanced at the clock, ten minutes past the hour, twenty minutes since he walked in the door, plenty of time to allow his anxiety to manifest.

She lit a cigarette, thinking about what this one might be like, feeling her passion for the play start to materialize. She liked this moment, savoring the potential as she inhaled the white-blue smoke and contemplated what may lie in store. She never knew exactly what would happen, that was part of it, no scene was ever the same, the agendas that they carried were always open to a myriad of interpretations, her moods and enjoyments changed rapidly, creating quirky nuances and twists that added to the overall composition.

Stubbing out the lipstick-stained butt, she turned and her seven-inch heels took her down the hallway to her destination.

The sharp clicking of her stilettos could be heard in the room where he waited, each step bringing them nearer to their fate.

June 21, 2001: The Escape Artist

The stars kissed the earth as enchanted night coursed down upon infinite and sightless black leather. He had been in bondage for days, although he could not recount how many moons had shone, how long the planet revolved around his solitary incarceration. Like an infant in a cradle, notions of time had been reduced to the basest of human needs: food, fluids, sleep.

I had warned him in a voice as smooth and scalding as a lava flow, with words as beautiful, as deadly. Heated words, molten to touch—"Kidnap," "Inescapable," "Forever"—words that warmed the very core of his sexuality, of his heart, words he had dreamed but never truly believed.

Our relationship was more akin to fairy tales than the cool rigidity of truth, carrying hidden meanings in all directions, spinning archetype and fable and dream to create the intricate ties that bound his being to the ecstatic rituals of power. Truth was subjective, each role bringing a new genuineness, collaborative fabrications becoming more pertinent than tangible reality.

In a world where dreams function as reality, how can one trust that words will not evaporate like the stars of dawn?

I had warned him. Now his head, locked in a greasy leather hood that prevented the intrusive sounds of the world, echoed my lurid words. He replayed the Grand Guignol; how I had led him down the path, how eager he had been to play the serenade of games, how careless he had been to step through the looking glass.

The leather interior of the hood was wet with his ocean-water tears. He struggled against the eternal ties that bound him. Attempted to scream through the soiled panties that I had forced into his desiccated mouth and secured with gummy silver duct tape and crude jute rope.

I had called it a game, tying him up and watching him escape, watching his moves, studying his form as he pulled at ropes, twisted his svelte body, untied knots with his toes. Proudly he would attempt to show his skill. As the months passed, my bondage became more efficient; perhaps he should have noticed, but I distracted him with promises, motivated him to escape from more and more difficult situations: "Houdini, break out of this bondage and I will let you worship my . . ."

And then there came a time when he could no longer escape, when I had learned all his moves, when there were no more tricks up his sleeve. There came a time when fifty-foot lengths of five-eighth-inch rope and inflatable leather hoods and impervious locking chains and sturdy satin bodybags all worked in placid solidarity to shroud any hope of freedom.

How long ago that was he did not know, he only knew what I put in his mouth, the smell of my hair, how the ropes no longer moved to his will, and that dreams can come true.

Scene Notes with
Mistress Mona

MISTRESS LEIA FEYHEART

I am an idiot, I say to myself as I climb the stairs to Mistress Mona's Mansion. I am dragging a suitcase of toys that I am almost certain would best serve now as a boat anchor. What kind of an idiot drags a suitcase with four hundred feet of rope to a dungeon noted for its thousands of feet of beautiful hand-worked hemp? Me . . . I'm that kind of idiot.

I am a woman who is dominant in all my kink and, to be honest, in every other part of my life, except for the several hours a month I submit to the dominant sadism of Mistress Mona. Have to have my rope and toys so everyone knows I'm really serious. How else would anyone know? Clever girl, do you think, maybe, you feel a little insecure just before the trip to the bottom?

Great, here I am climbing stairs in a long stupid green dress and dress coat and high heels with my stupid boat anchor thumping with each step up, trying to drag me backwards. For the fifth time since I started to climb the stairs to her doorway I step on my skirt, and it threatens to slip from my hips and fall to the ground. I wonder if anyone will notice me tumbling down the front of this grand old Victorian with a huge queer flag flying over my head, being dragged head over heels. Skirt serenely lying on the top step like a fallen green leaf on the peach-colored steps of my mistress's dungeon. That will, I finally decide, nicely address my exhibitionist desires, but not impress my mistress's neighbors. I always make a sincere effort to slip unnoticed past them, each time I march to her dungeon or stagger away an hour or two later. I decide, in a moment of perfect foresight, that even here on the fringes of the Castro, people will notice a naked, long-blond-haired woman in five-inch heels doing somersaults down a row of stairs, dragged by an eighty-pound bag of rope and kinky toys. With my luck, the bag will tear open, and I will be found by the paramedics tangled in piles of hemp, vaginal plugs, cock gags, and dildos.

I'm not even inside and I am already in a predicament.

How in the name of God do women manage in stupid heels and skirts, I ask for the thousandth time. Somehow I make it to the door and once again I am stunned by the pure perfection as I step into her château. Grand Italianate interiors from the School of Fontainebleau design seduce me into the dungeon.

Christmas has come and gone, and we are even into the new year, but candles still light the entryway wrapped by holly laurels, and beyond that, the Christmas tree. It lights up the far end of the entry hall, while the candlelight and chandeliers glisten off gold-leaf doors and the drumbeat of haute-red walls. Scents of warm oils and vanilla. The outside cold is forced away as I am warmed in my safe haven. This is the home of my mistress and I am welcome here.

Mistress Mona appears, an elfin queen, radiating power in her exquisite clothing and pure feminine presence. Strands of creamy pearls frame her lovely dark features. Her hug is warm and genuine and I think she must be as happy to session with me as I am to session with her. She has told me the special pleasure she takes when she tops a top. Good. Good. I follow her down the hall.

I decide to petition a favor. Please take my picture. I hand her my camera. I take a pose I practiced last night with my belly dance company. I have spent hours every day on my face and hair and exercising, hoping I will soon have some photos I am proud to show. I don't think Mistress Mona cares, she seems to treasure me regardless. Oh, that feels so very good. My tail makes a little wiggle.

She tells me she would like to see me in my corset. Oh no, oh no, I think; this is going too fast, she is going to corset me and then pierce my jutting breasts with needles again, and I twist with fear inside. I have accepted her needles before, and she is proud of me, because it scares me so. That fear is an issue to work with, a boundary to ease away, I hear her say.

A few moments later I look up into the mirror, and now, with the corset on, I look much more like a pretty woman. I get a little lost, looking at myself, beautiful in a certain way, when I notice she has moved onto the bed. I recognize the position; she intends to spank me.

I have seen her spank bottoms before and I think how lucky

I am. No needles. I slide onto her lap, putting all my weight on her thighs, with only my corset on, and she begins to spank me, warming the skin, loading me with endorphins. I feel almost hypnotized by the rhythm and the pace and begin to slip away from my body, floating. I am in heaven, I am a princess and I am being spanked by my queen. We are royalty.

No! This is a disaster! A sudden disaster. I don't know what to do, this has never happened before. Not from a spanking. Please no, I think to myself, please don't come on her knee. Not on her beautiful dress. My body betrays me, and uncontrollably, I am grunting and moaning, grinding my pelvis against her. I can't stop. Filthy, filthy animal. I strain to lift away and Mona forces me down. A moment ago I was royalty and now I am a nasty whore.

"Stop, Leia, stop," I scream to myself, but somehow in my transformation into a woman, I have become uncontrollably orgasmic, my vagina ready to seize. I am a cat in heat. I am appalled. "Show some control, Leia," I plead to myself, but great sexual energies take my body and use it. I am so sorry. If only I could stop coming, if only I could be good. I want to be good, but I come and come as my mistress spanks me. Moaning, thrusting, grunting, and grinding my pelvis into her beautiful black leather dress, I am coming over and over again, in rhythm to the strikes she delivers by hand. I'm sorry, I cry time and time again between the moans, but that nonsense is rebuked with burning hot strikes from my mistress, and I realize now that she controls me and she will do what she will. Submit, I say to myself, at least try to submit.

I am exhausted. How much time has passed, being spanked and coming? I have lost all track, maybe an hour, maybe a week, I can't really think. Finally she stops my torment and asks me to go to the front room and wait for her in front of the throne where she sometimes sits as I dance for her. I know she intends to cane me. I hate canes. I look around; beside me I see her ivory sheepskin rug in front of the fire.

She moves the punishment horse to the center of the room, between me and her throne. A certain dread begins when I realize she is going to restrain me. She lies out the thick black leather restraints for my wrist and ankles and then four padlocks. I'm afraid I may start screaming in fear, my chest tight, for she is going to really, really hurt me. Tie me up and then do anything she likes. Hurt me terribly. Why else would she chain me to the horse?

I could end it. I have a safe word. Caning. I hate canes. I am filled with fear and anxiety. Without question I am afraid and anxious enough to beg mercy, but we are making, well, art. I am an artist and we are creating beauty. How could I safe word that?

We are also creating trust, and from that forge the true bond in bondage. In my mind's eye I can see myself, creamy white skin, golden blond hair, bound in a black dragon-dressed corset, black leather restraints, chrome and brass locks, inescapably bound to leather, wood, and steel. My cheeks reddened by her hand. I see myself in my mind and I quiet. It is art, I think, I am beautiful.

My genitals lie exposed, I have become a thing, but Mona has made me a beautiful thing: female, available, desirable.

Men and women might lust for me if they could see what Mona has made of me. That is enough, I am content, I love this. Sweet music fills the dungeon as Verdi's *Dance of the Priest-*

esses comes to an end and Chopin's *Nocturne* begins to play gently in the background. I am royalty, I know it; I am a princess in disguise playing the games of royalty.

I relax into the music, my vision of myself, and the joy I see in Mona's eyes. I think to myself, this is what I do with my bottoms, too. I know what you are thinking, and what you are feeling—I will give myself to you so we can both live this dream and make our art. In this, I am able to submit. In this, you may dominate me.

The blows begin. It is a strap—straps are okay, I just hate canes. "I will cry no more than I must. In pain there is truth. I live in the moment. I am only . . ." What the hell is she doing now? My mistress has stopped strapping me and I can hear her spreading a pad on the floor under my pussy. A pad on the floor? Then, ominously, cold gentle movements around my vagina, around my clitoris.

And I am going to drip on the pad. You stupid, stupid girl, why did you tell her you had a phobia around cold steel speculums? Dear Lord, what is she going to do?

Unexpectedly, I feel a soft tingle. My mistress was just placing the vaginal plug that attaches to her Eros Tek.

I feel so relieved. No cold nasty speculum. No secret rite of Lesbian Pro Dommes, and no sudden gushing of some unidentified fluids, pooling on the floor under my pussy. I know what is happening! Mistress Mona is going to help me take the pain of the caning by using the Eros Tek. She is going to use the electronic stimulation to block the pain and the cane won't really hurt at all. She is so very good to me. She is taking good care of her girl. Mmmm, I rub my face against the red leather, she must really care about me. Lovely.

I begin to deliver the baby.

What a filthy trick! Wicked, evil, nasty, dirty, filthy trick. I never even had sex with a man until three days ago and now this. I don't want to have a baby.

In a moment of crystal clarity I realize I should have thought a bit before I e-mailed my mistress a lurid three-page account of renouncing my virginity with the other sex when I had my way with two men and two dommes with riding crops.

One minute ago I was feeling all safe and cherished and now she has me fucking pregnant and in labor. Contraction, contraction, contraction—oh my God!

Devil in a black dress and pearls! I'm chained facedown on a wooden horse and now I am in friggin' labor. The vaginal electrode fires again and again in perfect robotic rhythm, grabbing every muscle in my pelvis, and I am torn by the massive contractions.

I'm sorry, Mistress. This time I really mean it. I am so very, very sorry I sent that damned e-mail. "Breathe, Leia, pant like a dog, uugh—what else did they say to do? Think!"

Apparently my mistress has chosen for me to deliver to the gentle sound of Chopin, but that is odd, because I remember my mistress had told me she likes to cane to Chopin. Oh yeah, I remember now, this was all about caning. I hate canes.

She shows me her cane. Instantly, I hate it.

Actually she has done a good job of relieving my anxiety about the caning. I don't care about the goddamned cane, I'm having a baby. Yes, probably that is the kindest cane you own. You will not hurt me more than I can bear.

Edge play. I might define it as being chained to a punishment horse while having massive birth contractions three days after your first sex with a man, and having your mistress whisper that you must beg for a caning. I would ask for the caning but the words are trapped in my throat. I am so afraid. Afraid of the cane, afraid I will disappoint Mistress Mona, afraid I cannot submit. Afraid there really has to be a goddamned baby up there forcing its way out. With juicy stuff. That damned pad. What else does she know that I don't?

I can't complain, she told me she was a sadist, I just forget between sessions. I have no right to feel betrayed, but I yell out in fury anyway, explosively, accusingly, "You are a sadist!" She is so surprised she laughs, not loudly, but genuinely.

Edge play. I am an edge player. I pride myself in that. Finally, I ask her for the strokes, and the wrath of the goddess blazes across my buttocks. As my screams come, first with the contractions and then with the cane, an icky thought wiggled into my mind and I try to change the pitch of my howls. They had not been, after all, in key with Chopin, and this is, well, Art.

Only someone who has been caned can understand what it feels like. The cane hurts enough, and later, I cry. I cry not in pain or humiliation, but because I must leave, our time over. I dress reluctantly, demands on me pulling me into the real world, where life is always so much less intense that I never feel fully alive and nothing is quite as beautiful.

Lip Service

CECILIA TAN

aley cinched her belt tight, settling the metal tip of the end through the buckle with a click. In the dim light from the ubiquitous torchiere lamp in the corner, she turned first one hip, then the other, toward the mirror. The pants were tight, the supple leather straining at the crotch seams. So what, Haley thought, the corners of her mouth tugging down for an instant. Ten pounds or ten cigarettes a day, those are your choices.

She snapped her leather vest closed over bare breasts and snugged the leather cap down onto her head. Now, if I can just get my boots on, I should be fine.

A light snow had started falling, so the first thing she did when she walked into the Spur was to dust herself off, brushing at the hard-polished leather sleeves of her jacket with her gloved hands. Then she looked around. The Spur was dark, too dark really to see, which she never understood, since wasn't cruising really dependent on eye contact? Not that Haley cruised here; the Spur was a men's bar. She just came here sometimes, as if by being here some of that old leather musk would rub off on her. Tonight, though, was different. Tonight she had a mission.

She walked slowly in the almost opaque darkness, to the puddle of slightly brighter light by the empty pool table, and then to the bar, where she got herself a hard cider. As she put her lips to the bottle, though, she couldn't help but picture something else in her mouth: Mistress's cock. Actually, Mistress had several cocks, in varying colors and shapes, but the one she preferred to ram into Haley's mouth was pseudorealistic. A shovel-pointed head bulbed at the top of a six-inch-long shaft, very realistic except for the swirl of pink and purple that was its color. Haley had been blindfolded the first few times she had knelt at Mistress's feet and sucked cock. So it hadn't been entirely fair when Mistress had unveiled it yesterday in its technicolor glory, and Haley had laughed out loud. It was that laugh that had gotten her sent here tonight.

Haley watched men move from one side of the bar to the other. On one wall's large-screen TV, young buff men fucked each other. In the one brightly lit corner of the place, the boot-black leaned against his riser, waiting for a customer. Once in a while a man would go down the stairs, or come up them—kind of like sharks circling, Haley thought—like they'll die if they stop moving. How was she supposed to approach one of them?

It was early yet, the crowd thin. In the summer, after the

bar closed at two, everyone would mill around outside until three in the morning or later, the cruising going on at curbside as if nothing had changed. They called it the Sidewalk Sale, which Haley found too funny. But tonight, with snow coming down, who knew if things would get busy, or if it would stay like this? She knew she shouldn't dawdle in her task, but how to start?

She decided to get her boots shined while she worked up her nerve, though in the end that made it easier. Some boot-blacks were like some hairdressers: chatty. This one was any-way. While he was brushing down the sides of her motorcycle boots, he said, "So, whatcha doing hanging around the Spur anyway?" And, though she blushed to her roots, Haley an-swered, "My mistress sent me out to learn to suck cock."

"That right?" he replied, as if he heard that sort of thing every day. Maybe he did. "Well, come to the right place, you did."

"Got any tips?" she asked, trying to sound nonchalant about it.

"Eh, well, toughest part's knowing when to be gentle, and when to be rough. Some guys like a little teeth. Others, slap you upside the head for it. Dunno. Depends on the guy, I guess."

Haley tipped him well when her boots were done. While she'd been sitting up there, a few more men had come in. She went back to the bar and waited for the bartender's attention. When he came around she decided it wouldn't be so difficult. She thought: What do I have to lose? "I'm trying to learn to suck cock," she said, when he was leaning over toward her.

"Excuse me?"

"My mistress sent me. To learn to suck cock." She raised her eyebrows in an "Is that okay?" expression, and he smiled.

"Well, you want to see it done, be downstairs around midnight." He winked. "If you're in a dark corner I don't think the guys will notice you. They might, you know, get self-conscious if they know a woman's there."

"No, really?"

He shrugged. "Hard to say. Some nights it doesn't happen. But sometimes a kind of group grope gets going down there . . . we have to break it up of course. But sometimes it goes on for a while . . ." He gave another shrug, a coy one this time.

Group grope, eh, Haley thought. You wouldn't find a bunch of lesbians crowded into a dark corner of a bar sticking their hands into one another's panties. Or if you do, I've been going to the wrong bars.

Haley got another cider and staked out a place at the top of the stairs. A really straight-seeming guy in a suburban-looking leather jacket and loafers went down the stairs and Haley wondered what his story was. Haley'd had exactly three sexual experiences with men, none of which were really worth mentioning. And she'd had countless vanilla lesbian encounters in college, which were equally undeserving of mention. And then she'd met Mistress.

It hadn't happened like she'd thought it would. She had started hanging out at the Spur after she discovered leather, waiting for the dykes to show up. But they never did, and Haley really began to wonder if there were any leather dykes outside of the fabled promised lands of San Francisco and New York. She'd tried the munches, the meetings, no dice. So she had saved up her money and nerve, and called a woman who advertised in the weekly newspaper. That was how it started. Mistress was 100 percent woman, 100 percent femme, and 100 percent in charge, which was all that mattered to Haley in the end.

When they were together, it was easy to submit. It felt graceful and natural when Haley was overwhelmed by her presence and enveloped by her power. Which was why, she knew, Mistress sent her out on this solo excursion, to see what she would do without Mistress's hand there to push her along. Haley took another swig of her cider, her throat tightening as she thought about what she was supposed to do. She wasn't sure that she could.

What would the punishment for failure be? She swallowed hard, knowing suddenly, even though Mistress hadn't said so, that the punishment would be banishment until the task was done. Mistress never spoke about punishment or failure. She merely expected success, and therefore usually got it.

Haley put her empty bottle on the bar and went down the stairs.

She found a dark corner, though every corner was dark, and sat there, watching the men watching each other. Down here very few men spoke to one another, though some of them seemed to know each other. Mostly they just . . . stood. Haley, who had no watch, had no idea when midnight came or went. She thought she understood, though, why the Spur chose to play throbbing nonvocal disco music. She felt herself almost fall into a trance as the men around her also waited.

A hand on her shoulder jolted her awake. Someone with beer breath spoke in her ear. "Hey, Jock upstairs tells me you need some help."

"Uh . . ."

"C'mon."

She turned to see a short man with hunched shoulders walking away from her. He looked back over his shoulder, an unlit cigar clenched in his teeth, his own leather cap pulled down tight over his eyes. His bare arms looked skinny sticking out of his leather vest and his jeans were blue. She followed him.

He skirted around a wooden St. Andrew's cross, and went through a narrow open doorway.

Beyond the door was a tiled and grimy wall, lit with blue and striped with a long mirror. To the right were a line of beat-up-looking black bathroom stalls. As she caught up to him, he swung the door open on one and made an "after you" gesture. He didn't follow her in, however. He swung the door shut behind her, where it stuck in the crooked stall.

"Sit down," he told her.

She undid her belt and pushed the too tight leathers from her hips, sat down, and recycled all that used cider. She was looking for the toilet paper when she noticed the glory hole.

"That's right," came his voice through the hole.

"Why didn't I think of that?" Haley wondered aloud. She knew about glory holes, though she wasn't sure just when she'd come into that bit of knowledge. She couldn't see him through the hole, nor see his boots underneath, but she could hear him in there.

"Tell me what you're expecting," he said. "I'll talk you through it."

Haley sat there with her cunt dripping while she talked, which seemed appropriate somehow. "I guess, I guess I'm expecting something like a dildo, only warmer."

His chuckle was high-pitched. "Okay, that sounds about right. So you're sitting in there, and in through the hole comes a live flesh dildo. The guy on the other end has his hand around his balls and he waves it at you. What do you do?"

"Uh, I put it in my mouth."

"How? Do you just open wide and clamp down, or what?"

"No, no, I guess I'd . . . sort of lick it first. To lube it up, a little."

"What's it taste like?"

Haley closed her eyes. "It's salty. It's salty and it smells a little like yeast, bready."

"Where the hell did you get that idea?"

"Gay porn," she answered. Probably where she first heard about glory holes and leather bars in the first place. It was what she used to think about while her girlfriend licked her between the legs in a creaky dorm room bed.

Again the chuckle and, "You crack me up." His exhale was harsh. Haley realized he was masturbating, which only made her want to slip her own fingers between her legs. "Okay, so it tastes like salt and dough. Then what?"

"Then I lick some more, all the way around the . . . the head. And then I get my tongue underneath and let the head into my mouth."

"Like an oyster on the half shell."

"Uh, I guess," she said, trying to recall the feel of a salty, rubbery oyster in her mouth. But oysters were usually ice cold.

"Then what?"

"Then . . . then I start to suck."

"No, this is when you get good," he said, then chuckled,

having cracked himself up with his joke. "How much do you take?"

"I take . . . three inches. I rock my head forward and back, letting my lips tighten over the ridge where the head widens out."

She didn't think of this as a submissive game, but it was definitely a game. She heard more harsh breathing from the adjacent stall and went on. "As he starts to get more excited, I do it faster."

He squeezes his balls harder, and presses himself against the wall.

"I'm taking as much of him in as I can. I'm moving my head faster, squeezing harder. I'm wiggling my tongue, too. I'm going faster . . ."

"Close your eyes."

"What?"

"Close your eyes. No, move over the hole, then close your eyes."

Haley swallowed hard and licked her lips. She closed her eyes, trying to imagine Mistress standing over her, whip in hand, tried to imagine Mistress encouraging her . . .

"That's it, that's it. A little closer."

She edged forward. She could hear rustling now, and the hollow sound as her face drew near to the hole. Her heartbeat loud in her ears as she realized she was going to go through with it.

"Closer. Open your mouth."

Haley opened her mouth, her tongue protruding slightly and making her think of the dentist's office. Say ahhh.

"Here you go. Just move in a little."

Haley leaned forward bit by bit, as drops of her piss dried on her cunt and the sounds of what could only be the group grope outside reached her ears. Haley reached her tongue out farther, and leaned, and then felt something brush the edge of her cheek. She turned and her mouth closed over something shovel-headed and familiar and silicone. She sucked it in, taking as much of it in as she could, suddenly enveloped in Mistress's power once again.

"That's right, suck it," came the voice. "Take it all."

Haley sucked her Mistress's cock with a whimper. She sucked until she lost track of time, until a voice said, "Okay, guys, break it up in there." She opened her eyes to the white circle of the flashlight moving across the tile grid of the floor.

Her Mistress's cock hung on the glory hole toward her, the pink swirl turned lavender in the bluish light. Once she had pulled up her pants and gone around the other side, she found the stall empty. She pulled the dildo out of the hole and tucked it into the inner pocket of her jacket.

The bathroom was vacant. Out in the basement, things had thinned out since the grope was broken up, as men moved on to homes in pairs or alone. There was no sign of the little guy from the adjacent stall. Mistress had many minions. Haley patted her pocket. She was going home with a partner tonight, and tomorrow she was sure Mistress would want to hear all about it.

Poker Night

LISABET SARAI

*I*t was just an ordinary door. Solid core, Yale lock, standard peephole, identical to all the other doors on the fourth floor of this unexceptional building on the corner of West 14th and B Street. So why was he sweating and trembling as though he stood before the gates of hell? No, that wasn't quite right. He knew the door led through damnation, to salvation. He craved the peace, needed to be redeemed. But he was, as always, afraid to take that first step.

His cock was already an iron bar in his worn jeans. His heart jackhammered against his ribs. Don't be a pussy, he told himself. Get on with it. His work-reddened knuckles hesitated, inches from the door. Without warning, it swung open. His heartbeat raced into overdrive. He could hardly breathe.

"Evening, Jack. I thought I heard you shuffling around out in the hall. Come on in, before I shock all my neighbors."

She was decent enough, with her miniskirt and the black lace bra that cradled her ample breasts. But Jack scurried into the apartment. He didn't want to be seen, though everyone in the apartment building was probably parked in front of the tube.

Helen stood with her back to the closed door, surveying him. He blushed and stared down at his work boots.

"It's been awhile, Jack. I was beginning to think you didn't want to see me anymore."

"Seven weeks, ma'am. I tried . . . tried to stay away. But I couldn't stand it." He was appalled to feel tears pricking the corners of his eyes. "I needed to see you."

Perceptive as always, she saw his distress. "Hey, don't cry!" She enfolded him in a brawny embrace, burying his face in her bosom. "It's okay. I understand." She smelled of Ivory soap and talcum powder. His swollen cock throbbed painfully, and for a moment he thought he'd come right there.

She released him in the nick of time. He stepped away from her, head bowed in embarrassment.

"How's Maude?"

"Fine," he mumbled.

"Does she know you're here?"

He gazed at his mistress, eyes full of pain. "Of course not. She thinks I'm over at the Moose Club, playing poker with the boys. Hey, I was, for more than two hours, before I came here." He stared at his hands, fighting the guilt. "I don't like to lie to her."

"Why don't you tell her the truth?"

"I can't. She wouldn't understand. She's the church organist, for heaven's sake. She teaches Sunday school."

"You told me that she likes sex."

"Sure she does, but only normal sex. Healthy, ordinary sex, insert tab A into slot B. You know what I mean."

"There's nothing unhealthy about what you and I do."

"Yeah, right." He gave a bitter laugh. "Well, I suppose there's no law against it. It's not like I'm a homo or anything."

"Nothing unhealthy about that either."

"Look, I don't want to talk about it, okay? Let's just get on with it."

Jack dug his wallet out of his pocket with difficulty, wincing as the denim stimulated his bulging prick. He pulled out a wad of bills and laid them on the television table. "Here. I was lucky tonight. Won more than a hundred bucks."

Helen looked at him, some unreadable expression on her broad features. Then she rearranged her face into a mask of authority. He could see it happen, the shift to her professional mode. He could hear it in her voice.

"All right, then. Into the dungeon, little boy."

She opened the door into what would have been the kids' bedroom, if Helen had kids. The nontraditional decor, familiar as it was, still shocked him. Heavy black curtains hid the walls and cloaked the one window, which faced onto the alley running between B and C streets. The yards of fabric muffled noise, making the room into a dark cocoon. The light was indirect and soothing, coming from several track fixtures installed in the ceiling.

The furnishings were homemade but effective enough. In

the center of the room was a punishment bench fashioned from two heavy-duty sawhorses—he knew the brand, popular with local contractors—and a plank padded with gardener's foam knee pads. Opposite the door stood a bondage rack made of steel conduit. In one corner was a sturdy old armchair she must have picked up from the Salvation Army, augmented by leather wrist and ankle restraints. Arrayed on the pegboard along the left wall (just like the one in his garage, where he stored his tools) were coils of hemp and cotton rope, clamps and turnbuckles, a rattan cane, several paddles of wood and rubber, and a vicious bullwhip. He knew that it was vicious. From experience. The plastic storage bins under the pegboard, spraypainted black to fit in with the decor, held more implements and supplies.

Jack hovered on the threshold of the dungeon, temporarily paralyzed by fear and excitement. She gave him a little push.

"Get going. Or I'll send you home to Maude."

He stumbled in and stood, slightly dizzy, in the middle of the room. Helen went over to rummage in the storage boxes. "Strip, boy," she called over her shoulder. "Now."

Jack kicked off his boots and unzipped his jeans. His heart was pounding again, so hard that it hurt. His cock surged as he dragged his pants off. His fingers fumbled at the buttons on his flannel shirt. He was down to his underwear when she turned back to him, her arms full of paraphernalia.

"What? Not naked yet? Get a move on, boy!"

Hurriedly, he pulled the undershirt over his head, exposing his broad, hairy torso. The stretchy cotton undershorts snagged on his swollen prick as he wrestled them off.

"Get over to the rack." Her palm landed on his pale butt

cheek with a resounding smack. That single hot, sharp blow nearly sent him off. He tightened his muscles in alarm, struggling for control. If he shot his wad without her permission, she'd beat him till he couldn't sit for days. That always made Maude suspicious.

Helen secured his wrists to the upper crossbar, but left his ankles free. She circled his stretched body, appraising his state of arousal, making her plans.

"So, you were playing poker tonight?"

"Yes, ma'am."

"Did you drink a lot of beer?" He knew right then what her nasty game was going to be. His cheeks burned with the understanding.

"Some, ma'am."

"How much, boy?"

"Three cans of Bud, ma'am."

"Not enough. Drink this." She poured a big glass of water and held it to his lips. He realized that he was quite parched, and drank greedily. She refilled the glass. "Again."

He could feel the liquid settling in his gut. "I can't . . ."

"What did you say, boy? Why are you here if you're not going to obey me?" Her anger melted him, then brought him to a boil. He drank two more glasses.

"Good. Now, my little boy, I know that sometimes you can't control yourself. But I have what you need."

She picked up something white. It was an old-fashioned cloth diaper, but on a giant scale, big enough to fit a six-footer like Jack. He wondered briefly where she had found it. Unlike most of her equipment, this wasn't something they sold at Home Depot.

"Spread your legs, baby." The soft cotton caressed his rigid prick, making him moan. Her fingers were cool on his sweating flesh as she pinned the thing at each hip.

She stood back to admire her handiwork. He blushed again, aware that he must look ridiculous, embarrassed to realize that this simply made him hornier. "Very good. But I'll need something pretty strong, won't I, for you to feel it through that thick diaper?" She retrieved the cane from the wall. "This should do the trick." The flexible rattan rod whistled through the air as she warmed up. The hair at the back of his neck stood on end at the sound. His balls tightened into aching knots.

"Open your thighs wider. And bend over so the fabric's stretched tight across your butt. That's good."

Jack trembled, off-balance, waiting for the first stroke. Leaning forward, he found that the padded cuffs around his wrists supported most of his weight. Then again, he felt as though the lump of granite jutting from his crotch would be heavy enough to drag him to the floor. He had been hard half an hour before he left the game, knowing that this would be his final destination. He hoped nobody had noticed his hard-on when he got up to leave. Early delivery at the store, he had told them. Need to get my sleep.

All the last week he'd been harried by anxious dreams, but he'd sleep soundly tonight. He always did, after a session.

"Ready, baby?"

"Yes, ma'am," he murmured. Still the pain surprised, biting into his flesh as though his ass was totally bare.

"Ow!" he yelled. He had time for two deep breaths before she slashed at him again. His cock jerked against the cotton that bound it against his belly, threatening to explode. The cane left tracks of fire burning across his buttocks. The agony spread and mutated, merging with the awful pressure in his bladder. Each searing stroke hurt more than the last. He was shaking, near tears, from the excruciating pain and the effort of staying in control. Yet when she paused to catch her breath, he craved another stroke. The pain was almost unbearable, but its loss was even worse.

She might have read his mind. "Enough, baby?"

Jack was silent, overwhelmed with shame. He didn't want to admit it, his weakness, his sickness.

"Answer me, boy. Have you had enough of my cane? Or do you want more?" The authority in her voice sent a delicious chill up his spine. Did it even matter what he wanted? He was in her power. Everything was up to her.

"No answer. I guess that means you're done, that you can't take any more . . ."

"No . . . More . . ." The croaking voice seemed to belong to someone else.

"What was that?"

"More, please, ma'am. Give me more."

Her mocking laugh shriveled him. It hurt more than the cane. Yet strangely, even though his erection sagged, he was still excited. His balls were still tight. His bladder was as swollen as his cock had been, and somehow that turned him on, too.

"It's hard to admit that you're such a kinky little baby, isn't it? That you like it when I beat you. But it's okay. That's what I'm here for, to give you what you're afraid to ask for from any-one else. Let's check your marks. See if I think you can take any more. We can't send you back to Maude with your butt looking like barbecued chicken."

The mention of his wife's name made him squirm. She knew that, Helen did. It was all part of the performance.

Just because he understood didn't mean that he failed to react. She stood behind him, close to his suspended bulk. He could feel the heat coming off her body, smell her talc and a hint of oceany woman-scent. She barely touched the edge of the diaper covering his ass. The welts on his butt screamed as the cloth moved against them. He sucked in his breath, struggling once again for control. The urge to pee was unbearable. Gently, Helen peeled the cotton away from his wounded skin.

"Hmm. Very dramatic. I know you're a tough guy, but I think you've had enough for tonight."

Jack was about to protest, to swear that he could endure another dozen strokes. She cupped his butt cheeks in her cool palms, and squeezed lightly. Echoes of the cane's agony raced through him. He screamed. His back arched. His legs turned to rubber. For a moment, he forgot to tighten the muscles controlling his bladder.

The pungent odor of urine filled the dungeon. Jack began to cry. He flinched as Helen landed a vicious slap on his lacerated ass. "Oh, you naughty baby! You've wet yourself again. Naughty, naughty! Now I'm going to have to change you. Then, I'm going to punish you."

She unbuckled the wrist restraints and massaged his shoulders to stimulate the blood flow. Her touch brought the blood back to his cock as well. The soaked cloth clung to the growing bulk of his erection, a guilty pleasure that made him harder still.

"But for now, I'm going to let you stand there in your wet diaper and think about what a bad baby you are."

Helen stepped out of her skirt and unfastened her bra. She wore no panties. Jack watched from under lowered eyelids, admiring her fair, freckled skin and ripe body. A bushy tangle of red-gold curls decorated the place where her solid thighs met. Fat, juicy-looking nipples crowned her pendulous breasts. She seated herself in the armchair, spreading her thighs a bit. Subtle musk mingled with the sharp stink of his pee. "Come here, boy," she ordered.

He was at her feet in a moment. After fumbling with the safety pins for a while, she gave up and yanked the soaked diaper down to his knees. He groaned as the cloth rasped over his welts. His cock sprang out, fully hard again.

Helen reached out to pinch the purple skin stretched over the knob with her lacquered fingernails. "What a nasty boy you are! Well, I know how to handle nasty boys." She patted her thighs. "Over my knee. Now."

Trying to hide his eagerness, Jack draped himself across her lap. Helen was a big woman. His feet reached the floor, but just barely. He spread his legs to brace himself, and she trapped his erection between her thighs.

"Like that, do you? Well, let's see whether you like this."

Her cupped palm landed solidly on his ass, directly on top of one of his stripes. He yelled and jerked his hips away. His captured cock rubbed against the silky skin of her inner thighs. Pain and pleasure twisted together, racing through his body and leaving him helpless.

"Breathe," murmured Helen. "This is going to hurt."

She spanked him, hard, first with one hand, then the other. The sting of her slaps was bad enough, but she deliberately aimed her strokes so they'd reawaken the agony of his caning.

Jack writhed against her, trying without success to escape the pain. She gripped him around his waist and rained furious blows on the tender skin of his butt cheeks.

"You should see your ass, boy," she gasped, breathless from her exertion. "You're red as a lobster. Can't even see the marks of the cane anymore. Everything's a nice, even scarlet." She aimed a few more slaps at his punished flesh, then stopped. She was clearly getting tired.

His skin burned and his muscles ached, but to be free from her blows was still a blissful relief. He lay in her lap, panting, more and more conscious of his swollen cock poking between her thighs. He moved a little, stealthily trying to increase the contact with her firm body, and was rewarded with another slap.

"Oh, you evil little boy! Trying to get off, are you?"

"Yes, ma'am." He couldn't hide anything from Helen. She knew him, better than anyone did.

"Get up. Let me see you." Awkwardly, he worked his bulk backwards, off her lap, gritting his teeth as his cock repeatedly brushed against her body. Finally he was kneeling at her side, his rigid prick swaying and pointing up at the ceiling. She reached down and squeezed it, hard. He closed his eyes and held his breath, struggling for control.

"Well, you've managed to hold on through some heavy stuff. Maybe you deserve to come. Would you like that?"

He didn't dare raise his eyes, but he knew she could see his smile. "Oh yes, ma'am. Please, let me come."

"Okay, you can come. But you have to jerk yourself off using your wet diaper."

"Oh, no, please, ma'am! Not that! I can't! That's disgusting!" Disgusting or not, his cock ratcheted up another few degrees toward the vertical at the thought.

"It's that, or I'll send you and that proud erection home right now." It was no good pleading. He knew that. "Come on, Jack." Her voice held a new hint of intimacy and complicity. "Don't disappoint me. We both know you want it."

He crawled over to the crumpled pile of fabric that lay near her feet. The smell was strong. He raised himself onto his knees, spreading his thighs for balance. Mastering his revulsion, he grabbed the diaper and wrapped it around his cock. The damp cloth clung to his flesh, cool against his fevered skin. He took a deep breath, trying to ignore the odor and all the shameful memories it awakened, and gripped his cock in strong fingers.

The diaper wouldn't slide. There was too much friction. It hardly mattered. Helen was watching him, leaning forward eagerly, lips parted, nipples taut, thighs open. One more squeeze was all it took. Pleasure, untainted by pain, overwhelmed him. His whole body convulsed. Milky fluid spurted from his spasming cock, showering Helen's toes. He closed his eyes and felt all the tension, the rage, the fear, the shame, the self-disgust, flow out of him, leaving him empty and at peace.

"Clean me off." Helen's voice, gentle despite its message of command, broke his reverie. As though in a trance, he bent and began to lick his cum off her white feet. He didn't mind the bitter taste. Long after he had consumed every drop, he continued to lap at her warm, fragrant flesh, dipping his tongue into the crevices between her toes, tracing the smooth arch of her instep.

"Enough." Helen raised him up until his face was level with

hers. "Enough." She bent and kissed him with closed lips. "Get dressed. I'll wait in the living room." Then she was gone. Jack groaned as he clambered to his feet and looked around for his clothes. The muscles in his thighs and shoulders were sore. His buttocks were on fire. He couldn't stand the tightness of his undershorts, though the rough denim created its own special agony against his punished flesh. Every step reminded him of Helen and his degradation.

He smiled when he saw her, sitting in front of the TV watching the late news. She had put on a flowered housecoat, exactly like something Maude would wear. His heart swelled with something, something that actually felt quite a bit like love. He fished another twenty out of his pocket and added it to the pile of cash. "Thank you, Helen. I really appreciate it."

She laughed. "Wait till tomorrow, Jack, when the pain really kicks in. You might not be so grateful!"

"No," he said softly. "I will."

She stood up to see him to the door. She patted his shoulder and kissed his cheek. "So, Jack. What will you tell Maude?"

A smile lit his middle-aged features, making him suddenly handsome.

"I'll just tell her that I had a lucky night."

Double Dipping

N. T. MORLEY

She caressed his face as it rested in her lap. He kissed her thighs now and then. He was sprawled across the bed, naked, his cock hard. Her hand lazily stroked it, caressing the engorged flesh enough to torment him, but not to get him off.

He never got off until she decided it was time, and she wasn't ready to let him off the hook just yet. He had been hard for an hour, his cock—and frequently his mouth—begging for release, but she wouldn't allow it until she was quite finished with him. Though it was the end of their paid hour together, that only served, in her mind, to release her from her obligations as a professional dominant. Now the fun could really begin.

"You'd do just about anything for me, wouldn't you?" she sighed rapturously.

"Yes, Mistress," he said. "Anything at all."

Caroline smiled, saying mischieviously, "Anything?"

Brian answered quickly, "Yes, Mistress. Anything."

"Be careful what you promise," she said. "Because I'll take you up on it."

Brian's head came up out of Caroline's lap, the eyes deep with submission and dull with arousal.

"Anything, Mistress," he said. "Anything you command."

He was a treasured client, visiting Caroline almost once a week for three months now. She would hate to push things too far and lose him.

But Caroline was never the sort of girl who could play it safe, and she was incredibly turned on right now.

She was in her twenties, a slim Asian girl with coal-black hair and a sprinkling of tattoos up and down her arms, legs, and back. She was not the typical dominant. She did not have a dungeon, just a cramped fourth-floor walk-up in Manhattan. She didn't have a complicated array of fetish outfits or an extensive collection of toys.

She dominated her clients with her hands, her nails, her teeth, her filthy and abusive mouth.

She dressed up for sessions by climbing into the same thing she'd wear on the street: tight jeans and tight T-shirts, bicycling shorts and sports bras, army pants and a wife-beater. Right now she was wearing what she'd wear to the supermarket, minus the jeans: a cotton thong, dilapidated black combat boots, and a white baby-T with the logo of a punk band scrawled across it. Brian could see her tits through the well-worn fabric.

She did scenes right there on her bed, the same place she

slept and dreamed, the same place she watched TV, the same place she wanked, frequently right after sessions and sometimes right before.

The same place she made love to whomever it pleased her to make love to.

The smile on Caroline's face was wicked, evil. She knew because she'd practiced it in the mirror, even though she really didn't need to. She practiced it because it made her wet.

"My new boyfriend lives on the third floor," she said. "He wants to be your boyfriend, too."

She saw Brian's eyes flicker with fear, a sight that gave her an intense heat between her legs, something she'd come to love about Brian in the last three months.

"Your boyfriend, Mistress?" he asked.

Caroline grinned and nodded. "Uh-huh. You sucked my dick so good last week, I think this guy should see what a good little girl you are. And if you do it *really* good," she added, slipping one long fingernail into her mouth and chewing on it, "maybe he'll fuck you as good as I fucked you last time."

Brian gulped. Caroline had indeed fucked him last time, making him suck her strap-on while she called him a little cocksucking slut. When he'd moaned in arousal at hearing that, she'd told him she was going to turn him into a queer, going to make him fuck boys. Then she'd flipped him over and done his ass good, which had made him come hard, and made her so wet she hadn't even bothered to put a towel down before he shot all over her favorite pillow.

"Yeah," smiled Caroline. "What, you think I'm not good to my word?"

"No, Mistress . . . I had forgotten."

"Well," she said. "I never forget. Go get me the phone."

It was Caroline's way of giving him one last out; if he balked at retrieving the cordless phone, she would let him off the hook. She would throw him over her lap, spank his ass for disobeying an order. Tell him she was disgusted with him and then send him away. They'd never speak of it again, and she wouldn't get to make Brian fuck boys.

But Brian didn't balk. He meekly got off the bed and went across the room.

The apartment was so small that it wasn't a long trip; Caroline's king-size bed took up practically the whole single room, which also featured the front door and the window that led to the fire escape. If she had lived in a one-bedroom, requiring Brian to be gone for even an instant, Caroline would have slipped her hand into her thong and given herself a good stroke before Brian returned. She was so horny she wouldn't have been able to stop herself.

But there would be plenty of time for that. Brian held out the phone for her and then obediently took his place across the bed, his head in her lap.

Propped up on pillows, Caroline stroked Brian's face.

She dialed a number quickly, from memory. Brian shivered underneath her as the phone connected.

"Yeah, hi, it's me," she said. "Listen, I've got a client here, and I think he's a little fucking cocksucker. I really want to find out for sure. Can you come over?"

"Yeah," came the response, loud enough for Brian to hear it.

"Hope you're good and horny!" said Caroline with a perky sound to her voice, and Brian looked up at her with a mixture of fear and excitement.

Caroline disconnected the call.

"He'll be right up," she said. "He really loves a good blow job."

Brian's eyes burned with a mixture of emotions. Seeing the conflict in them made Caroline even wetter than she was already. She knew she shouldn't be doing this, but she couldn't resist. She'd been waiting for this moment for months.

There was a knock on the door, and Caroline looked down at Brian, who stared up at her dumbly.

"Well?" she asked. "Aren't you going to get it? It's your new boyfriend."

Brian got up and went to grab his boxer shorts from the floor. Caroline made an annoyed sound and laughed in the infectious, disarming titter that always made guys think she was harmless. In fact, she tended toward more of a nervous giggle when she was really turned on, a mannerism that annoyed and embarrassed her no end but that guys seemed to like—she suspected because it made her seem girlish. Whatever the reason, she cultivated it in bed and tried hard not to do it out of bed. She'd gotten pretty good at it.

"Don't put your clothes on," she said to Brian. "It's nothing he hasn't seen." Her giggle again, and she could see Brian visibly reacting with pleasure at how cute she was. Go figure.

"Besides," she added, "he's coming over to fuck your face, the last thing you should be worried about is if he sees yours!"

Meekly, Brian dropped his boxer shorts and went to the door. The man was standing there in the hallway, a large African American with a bulge in his tight jeans. He looked like he worked out.

Brian just stood there, naked, in the doorway, in that awkward moment of two men meeting at the door of a woman's apartment. The new guy had a wry little smile on his face as he looked Brian up and down.

Caroline called from the bed, "Brian, this is Bruce. Bruce, Brian. Brian's going to suck you off, Bruce. Come on in and take your clothes off."

"With pleasure," said Bruce.

Brian went back to his place on the bed, his face in Caroline's lap. Bruce closed the door and stripped his shirt off over his head.

"Ever sucked dick before?" asked Bruce.

Brian swiftly shook his head.

"Well, you may as well start with the best," said Bruce, and unzipped his pants. His cock was thin but long, impossibly long. Brian's eyes widened.

"Kinda hard to get your mouth around it." Caroline giggled. "Trust me, I know."

Bruce kicked off his shoes, dropped his pants. He wasn't wearing underwear. He climbed onto the king-size bed on the same side as Brian.

"Nope," said Caroline with another giggle. "I want you on my side. Do it right over me. I want to see everything."

Bruce climbed over Caroline, letting his hard cock brush her belly as he did. Her hand went smoothly around it, gently stroking as he bent down to kiss her. Then he was over her, rolling onto his back, his big, hard prick still gripped in Caroline's hand.

Brian looked up at her in one last expression of dismay and excitement. Caroline looked down between Brian's legs and saw that his cock was hard.

"Come on," said Caroline. "You've gotten enough of them. You know what to do."

Brian leaned over Caroline and let her guide Bruce's prick to his mouth. He parted his lips gingerly, and Caroline could see the rush of shock as he tasted it for the first time. Bruce had a really drooly prick, and a lot of precum always glistened on the head. Caroline saw Brian tasting it, and it sent a heady rush of heat into her body.

"Yeah," said Caroline excitedly. "Now suck it deeper."

Brian obeyed, his lips sliding down the shaft of Bruce's cock as Bruce moaned softly. Caroline never took off her shirt during sessions, but now she couldn't stand the feel of the constricting baby-T covering her. She let go of Bruce's cock and stripped off her top. When she returned, Brian had put his own hand around Bruce's cock, his head bobbing up and down as he sucked it.

"Fuck," said Caroline. "I love to see a straight man suck cock."

She pressed her lips to Bruce's, her pierced tongue working its way into his mouth. Her hand went back down to Brian's face so she could feel his lips clamped tight around the shaft.

When her lips came away from Bruce's, she looked down at Brian and said, her voice like melted chocolate, "Now deep throat it, you little bitch. Take it all down your throat. You know I taught you how. Don't be coy. Take it all."

Caroline had, indeed, taught Brian how. She had taught him to take a deep breath and straighten his neck and relax his throat around the head of her dildo, then take it all down, right to the base. Something about doing it to a cock made it harder, though, and as Brian struggled to obey, Caroline saw him gagging and coming back up for air.

"Do I have to fucking spank you?" she snapped, her chocolate voice suddenly more like drain cleaner. "I'll fucking do it, Brian, you know I will! I want to see you swallow it all, you little cocksucker!"

Brian gave a little moan of arousal—always, from the beginning, the rougher Caroline spoke to him, the more turned on he got. In fact, it was having Brian as a client that made her such an expert in verbal abuse. That, and the fact that she'd found that nothing aroused her more.

Except seeing a straight man suck cock because she told him to.

Brian came up for air again, took a deep breath, and stretched his neck out. This time, Bruce's cock went right down, Brian filling his throat with it until his lips wrapped around the base of Bruce's shaft.

"Fuck," groaned Bruce. "This guy's a fucking born cocksucker."

Caroline planted her lips on Bruce's, her tongue plunging deep into his mouth while her hand stroked Brian's face, feeling his lips glide up and down on Bruce. She was so horny she wanted to scream. She finally couldn't take it anymore.

So absorbed were they that neither Brian nor Bruce noticed what she was doing. To be fair, it was a quick movement—she was pretty used to doing it on the fly. Her hands went to her cotton thong and swept it off her slim body in a single motion. Then she kissed Bruce hard again and pushed Brian off Bruce's cock.

"Fuck me," she told Bruce. Then, to Brian: "You. Get me ready."

She spread her legs wide, exposing her shaved and pierced

pussy as well as the tattoo of Betty Boop just above her clit. Brian only looked puzzled for an instant. He shifted his body slightly and his face descended between Caroline's thighs. He'd done this many times, and she'd taught him to do it exactly the way she liked it. His well-trained tongue worked wonders on her clit. The tip traced the piercings that ran down each lip, and when he focused on her clit Caroline almost came then and there.

But not yet. She pushed Brian away and snapped, "Kneel next to the bed," then spread her legs wider and put her arms around Bruce. Bruce didn't need any coaxing. He mounted Caroline easily and slid his cockhead between her lips, nuzzling her entrance. He entered her easily, making her gasp. She was so wet that it slid right in, droplets of juice even dribbling out onto his balls.

"Don't come," she growled into his ear as he began to fuck her.

Brian knelt beside the bed and watched, his cock throbbing hard as he saw Bruce's cock sliding in and out of Caroline. She dug her nails into Bruce's muscled ass and pumped her hips up to meet his thrusts. Caroline's coal black hair scattered across the pillow as she thrashed back and forth with the pleasure of her approaching orgasm. "Fuck me," she grunted. "Fuck me, fuck me, fuck me, fuck me, fuck me!" Then, "Harder!" she gasped as she reached her peak, the orgasm exploding through her while she wrapped her legs around Bruce and pulled him tight into her. He was so long that she could feel his cock head grinding against her cervix, feel the pressure on her G-spot, making her come even harder. She moaned in ecstasy as she finished coming, then pushed Bruce off her—something that would have been difficult to do for any other five-foot-one, eighty-five-pound girl.

"Finish him off," Caroline gasped, looking at Brian.

Her hand went around the base of Bruce's cock as he lay on his back and Brian took his place between Bruce's spread legs. This time, Brian did not hesitate; he seemed ravenous for cock. The sight of that made Caroline so hot she had to rub her pussy with her other hand. The aftereffects of her orgasm still went through her, little contractions in her cunt that made her whimper.

"Yeah, you like that, you little cocksucker," she moaned hungrily. "Swallow it all. Swallow all of his cum."

Bruce's hips began to pump as he got ready to shoot, and Brian rode him admirably, his mouth working up and down around the head so that when Bruce threw back his head and groaned, his lips were clamped tight so he could catch every drop. Caroline shuddered with arousal to know that Bruce's cum was shooting deep into Brian's mouth, pulsing down his throat. She rubbed faster. By the time Brian's mouth slowed on Bruce's softening cock, Caroline was right on the edge, ready to come, and all it would take was one small stimulus to get her there.

She kissed Bruce tenderly.

"All right," she told him with a glance toward Brian. "Your turn."

Bruce's eyes widened.

"Come on," she said. "You know you want to. Get up on the bed, Brian. You're not a real faggot yet."

Brian obediently climbed onto the bed, and Caroline guided him between her and Bruce. Caroline never got this cuddly with clients, but she couldn't stop herself. She wrapped her body around Brian's and snapped her fingers.

"Come on, Bruce, baby. Show Brian how much you appreciate his blow job."

Bruce looked sheepish, nervous, but he didn't refuse. Instead, he shifted on the bed, bent over, and took Brian's cock in his hand.

His tongue came out and swirled around the head, and then he took it into his mouth.

That was all it took. Caroline pressed her hand between her legs and in three short strokes it was over. She came so hard she barely knew what was happening; she writhed and surged against Brian, muttering "Jesus . . . Jesus . . . !" as she climaxed. When her eyes refocused, she saw Bruce hungrily gulping Brian's cock, his lips working the shaft while Brian arched his back, moaning as his ass left the bed.

"Don't swallow," sighed Caroline. "Hold it in your mouth."

Brian came with a groan, clutching at Caroline as if for reassurance. She wrapped her hand around the base of his balls so she could feel the pulses as Brian filled Bruce's mouth with cum.

Bruce came up from Brian's softening cock, his mouth full. Caroline smiled at him.

"Now kiss him," she said with a cruel smile. "Right on the lips. Open mouth and everything. I want to see both of you eat his cum."

Nervously, Bruce crawled up, trying to get between Caroline and Brian. She pushed him onto the far side of her, making the two of them share more skin contact. Bruce's legs twined with Brian's. Brian's wet cock drooled a string of cum across Bruce's thigh, which turned Caroline on even more.

The two of them kissed, gingerly at first, Bruce not opening his mouth.

She cleared her throat loudly. "Excuse me?" she snapped. "Who's in charge here?"

Bruce parted his lips, pressing his mouth to Brian's. Cum ran out of his mouth, dribbling down his chin and onto both their chests.

"Tongue! Tongue!" Caroline giggled.

Cum continued to run out of Bruce's mouth, but she could see their tongues wriggling together. She knew Brian had gotten a good strong taste, and it made her want to come again.

"Don't stop!" said Caroline when the two men tried to pull away from each other. "Not until I tell you to."

But there would be none of that. Not until the scene was over—how many times did she need to get off anyway?

After a half-minute of kissing, the men began to get more into it. Their tongues worked together, and when Caroline took Bruce's hand and planted it on Brian's cock, Bruce didn't pull away. He caressed Brian's soft organ gently, while the two of them kissed.

"Yeah," sighed Caroline. "That's what I like to see."

She stretched out on the bed, naked, energized. "All right," she told them. "You can go. Bruce, why don't you walk Brian to his car? That's what a gentleman does after a date." She giggled, her clit throbbing.

Bruce's mouth came off of Brian's, and the two men looked sheepishly at each other.

"All right," said Bruce.

"I'm . . . I'm just parked around the corner."

"It's not the best neighborhood," said Caroline, winking at

Bruce. "Walk him anyway. And be sure you give him a good-night kiss. Brian, you owe Bruce that, even if he didn't buy you dinner." She giggled. "And don't forget the tongue."

Both Bruce and Brian looked nervous at that, but Caroline saw in their eyes that they would obey. She stretched out on the bed and watched as the two men dressed in silence, then went to leave her apartment.

"And hold hands while you're walking," she said.

Brian and Bruce answered at the same moment, in one voice. "Yes, Mistress."

When the door closed, Caroline reached out to her night-stand and furiously dug for her favorite vibrator. As she touched it to her clit, she thought about the two men walking hand in hand, kissing on the street in full view of whoever was watching.

As she mounted toward orgasm, she took a moment to re-flect on her luck—two clients who had asked her, nay, begged her, to make them "go gay." Not just to talk to them about how they were little faggots or make them suck her strap-on. Not even just suck cock, anonymously, while she watched and, when you got right down to it, gave them permission. But ac-tually *do it* with another guy, swallow cum, kiss openmouthed, do it in public if possible. Make them kiss and grope and fon-dle *after* they'd left her apartment.

Two similar fantasies, two guys with the money to pay her for it. Double-dipping: ethically suspect, but sexually and fi-nancially excellent.

More important, Brian was the one client she knew she could control, and Bruce was the one client she'd been dying to fuck. Bruce had offered her a stunning sum of money to do exactly that with him. But if she'd just given in and fucked Bruce, what would that have done to their relationship? By humiliating him, the way he loved to be humiliated, it kept everything nice and simple. Or complicated, she supposed, in a way, but more important, it kept her in charge. That's what turned her on the most, that and watching guys suck cock, which was the only thing that truly sent her into the fucking stratosphere.

Besides, in an afternoon and early evening, Caroline had just made enough to pay for grad school.

Of course, if Bruce and Brian turned out to be gay, if her little psychodrama took them out of the closet . . . well, then she just lost *two* clients.

But it was worth it, she decided.

"Oh yeah," she moaned softly as she slid the vibrator into herself. She whimpered. "Oh yeah, it was worth it."

The Back of the Truck

GRETA CHRISTINA

"Honey, I'm home," I call out as I shut the door to our hotel room.

You blow me a kiss and continue jumping on the bed. "How was your day, dear?" you ask. "How was the gun show?"

"Not bad," I say, chucking some packages onto the dresser. "I met some guys from Sacramento who can get me some good stuff under the table. Not worth the trip, probably, but it's always fun to visit Frisco. What did you do while I was gone?"

"Slept, mostly," you say, flopping down on the bed. "The trip was exhausting. Oh, and I watched *Buttman's Aerobicise Girls* on pay-per-view, so don't be surprised when it shows up on the bill."

"You're awfully free with my money," I say. You shrug and yawn. "Yeah, whatever."

"So, are you still sleepy? Or are you ready to party?"

"Oh, party!" you squeal, kicking your heels. "Party, party, party! Where are we going?"

"Good," I say, tossing you a package. "Put that on. We have a date with destiny."

"Who's Destiny?" you ask as you rip into the paper bags. You shake out the contents: red fishnet thigh-highs, a red velveteen bustier, a black Spandex miniskirt, no panties.

"You are, my dear," I reply as you wriggle into the whorish outfit. "Now get your boots on." Someone knocks at the door. "Ah, that must be Jeeves now."

I open the door to Macius, who's wearing a cheap gray chauffeur's uniform rented from a costume shop. "Evening, madame," he says. "Hiya, slut-chick. You ready yet?"

"Yup," I reply. "Jerusalem, get your fuckin' boots on and let's go." We parade out of the hotel, and Macius leads us to my bright red Dodge pickup and opens the tailgate. "Hop in, slut-girl."

You scramble into the back of the truck and settle comfortably onto the foam rubber padding. There's actually a clean sheet for once, a garish red satin one, with creases from the package still in it. You touch the sliding glass separating the cab from the bed of the truck. "Mirrors? That's new."

"One-way glass," I say. "I had it installed while I was at the show. Thought it might come in handy. Now shut the curtains; I don't want you peeking. This is a surprise." I pull the curtains over the side and back windows, slam the tailgate shut, and crawl into the front. You squint at yourself in the one-way glass, and stick your tongue out as we rumble off into the night.

In just a few minutes, you can feel the truck pull into a parking space. I get out of the cab and open the tailgate. You start to crawl out, and I grab your arm and shove you back in. "Uh-uh. Stay there, cunt."

You peer out of the back of the truck. We are parked on a side street near a grimy, heavily trafficked thoroughfare. "Where the fuck are we?" you ask. "Where's the party?"

"We're just off Polk Street," I say. "The party's right here." I lean against the truck, assessing the scene on the street. "Yeah, we'll do okay. You're older than most of the kids here, but I think we'll get some action. Now get on your knees and stick your boobs out. We've got work to do."

You take a look around, at the red satin sheet and the seedy nightlife and the harsh light illuminating your trashy costume. "Daddy . . . no. Please. I don't like this party. I want to go home."

I look you over carefully. Without your usual bluster, the whorish outfit makes your wiry body look fragile and scrawny, a child playing dress-up in her mother's party clothes. My clit throbs. I always did have a thing for waifs. "Yes," I say. "Yes."

"No. Really. I don't want to do this, Daddy. I don't want all those strange ugly men sticking their dicks in me. Please don't make me."

I take your chin in my hand and force your face up to meet mine. You see my hunger, my compulsion. You see that watching the strange ugly men stick their dicks in you is exactly what I want. And you see me waiting for your safe word, the

I-mean-it-stop-everything-now safe word, the one you've never used. "Daddy, I'm scared," you murmur.

I stroke your hair. "I know you are, baby girl. But don't worry. I'll be right here. You get into any real trouble, just holler."

"You won't hear me."

"I sure will, baby face. I had an intercom installed, too. It's set on one-way; you can't hear me, but I can hear you loud and clear. Every squeal, every whimper. So whimper a lot for daddy. You know how much I like it."

Your eyes fill with tears. "Why do you do this shit? Why do you make me do things like this?"

"Because it makes my dick hard, darlin'," I reply. "We can discuss the deeper meaning later. Right now, I want you to suck the nice men's cocks. And do a good job. Remember, I'm watching you. Pretend it's me if you want."

I pause, waiting to hear the word that means you're walking, fed up for good. You keep your eyes on my face. You say nothing.

I smile, and lean against the truck. "Okay. Get into position, cunt, and let me do the talking. Here comes a live one."

You scramble onto your knees and arch your back, pressing your small breasts against the cheap fabric. A paunchy middle-aged man in white slacks and a yellow dinner jacket struts over to the truck. "Evening, ladies," he says pompously. He takes your chin in his hand and turns your head from side to side. "Now, what's a pretty little girl like you doing out on a night like this?"

"Talk to me," I say in a friendly voice. "She doesn't like to talk much." Yeah, right, I think. In my dreams.

"Oh, so you're her manager, are you?"

"Something like that. What are you looking for this evening?"

He thinks for a moment. "She has such a pretty mouth."

"I see." I nod. "Well, if her mouth is all you want, you can have it for twenty-five. Half an hour. You wear a safe, and we drive the truck. Just tap on the glass when you're done."

"Whaddaya mean, you drive the truck?" he bridles. "How do I know you won't take me somewhere and rob me?"

"We'll stay on busy streets," I answer. "You can peek out the window and keep track. Hell, give us the route if you like."

He stares at your tits, thinking it over. You give me a quick glance, then gaze into his eyes adoringly and lick your lips. You see his dick swelling in his trousers. "All right," he says. He peels off two tens and a five and climbs into the truck. I shut you in together and get in the front. You feel the engine rumble, feel the truck sway as it pulls into the street. The man begins to rub his dick through his pants. "Pull your skirt up, girly," he says.

You look at him, alarmed. "Hey, that wasn't part of the deal."

"Oh, I don't wanna fuck you." He chuckles. "I just wanna look. Come on, what's it gonna hurt you? It's not like nobody's seen it before. Come on, just pull it up and show it to me. I'm payin' for this."

You hesitate, then reluctantly comply. "That's a good girl," he says. He unzips his fly and pulls his dick out as you slowly roll your skirt to your waist. He reaches out, grabs your ass, and squeezes. Hard. You jerk away, and he quickly raps on the glass. I slide the window open. "Is there a problem?"

"Yeah," he says. "She won't let me touch her. I don't wanna fuck her or nothing, I just wanna touch her."

"You said you just wanted her mouth," I say. "You wanna touch her ass or her tits, that's another ten. You wanna stick your fingers in her, another ten on top of that." He sighs, reaches into his wallet, and hands me two more fives. "Okay?" he says.

"Jim dandy." I slide the window shut, and he reaches out and grabs your ass again. "Get on your hands and knees," he says. You obey, hating his guts. He kneels behind you and starts groping, squeezing your ass cheeks, reaching around to grab your tits, yanking your nipples, slapping your ass with his dick. The lurching movement of the truck throws you against him, and he gasps. "Turn around, girly. Turn around now and suck my dick."

You rotate around on your knees, groping for the bag of tricks we always keep in the truck. You slide a rubber on him, take a deep breath, and gulp his dick into your mouth. "I hope that bitch is enjoying this," you think as you slide your mouth over his cock. "Boy, am I ever going to make her pay for this. Twenty diamond necklaces. And another red dress. And a pony. At least." You look up at him worshipfully and slide your tongue in circles around his dickhead. "Just get it over with," you think. You feel his cock throb inside your mouth, and you shut your eyes, faking bliss. He grunts, and grabs you by the back of the neck, and comes, stuffing his dick deep inside your mouth. You cringe in disgust.

He starts to soften and shrink, and you sigh with relief. You strip the condom off, knot it, and toss it out the side window. He knocks on the glass. "Hey. We're done."

I slide open the window and watch him zip his pants back up. "You want us to drop you anywhere?"

"Uh . . . sure. Lombard and, um, Fillmore. I can walk to my motel from there."

"Okeydoke," I say, sliding the window shut. He unzips his pants again and idly rubs your face into his limp dick. You think about protesting, but decide it's not worth the effort. In a few minutes we pull up to his stop. "Enjoy your stay in San Francisco," I say, as he climbs out of the truck. "Come back real soon, ya hear?" He ignores me and wobbles off into the night.

You give me a look like a poisoned dagger. "I hope you enjoyed that, you rotten stinking hateful spider-bitch."

I grin, grab a handful of your tangled hair, and kiss you, choking your breath back, licking the taste of latex out of your mouth. "Oh, my Lord," I say. "You have no idea. You are so fucking beautiful. I had my hand down my pants the entire time. Ask Macius." Macius nods in vigorous agreement. "God, I want to crawl back there and fuck you myself. But I want to watch you more." I grab you around the waist and squeeze you tight, burying my face in your neck. "You make your daddy real happy. Let's go back to Polk Street."

You cling to me, savoring the comfort for once. "Did you really like it?"

"Sweet Mary, Mother of God. Yes. Yes, I liked it. I'll tell you all about it later. Let's go." I shove you back in and shut the tailgate, and we drive off again. You curl up on the cushions, soothed by the rumbling and swaying of the truck. You whine to yourself a little as you feel the truck pull into a parking spot . . . but you think of my eyes on you, watching you suck off these nameless strangers, and your pussy clenches, just a little.

I open the tailgate again, and you sit up and try to look pretty. We're back on our side street just off Polk. I stroke your hair idly, and we wait.

Two sailors approach, leering at you and nudging each other in the ribs. You give me an outraged look. "I am going to kill you," you say between your teeth. "I am going to take my brand-new Smith and Wesson and my brand-new bullets and shoot you in the twat." I laugh heartily and speak to the sailors. One is tall and blond, the other a short, stocky redhead. "Howdy, boys," I say. "Whatcha got cookin'?"

They nudge each other and giggle. "How much is she?" Red asks.

"Depends on what you want."

"What if I wanna fuck her up the butt?" Blondie says, and laughs insanely at his own witticism.

Red glares at him. "What are you, some sort of faggot?"

Blondie bridles. "I ain't no faggot. She's a girl, isn't she? I just wanna do her up the butt." He dissolves into guffaws once again.

"You want her up the butt, that's seventy-five," I answer. "You both want her butt, I'll give you a discount. One twenty-five for both."

"Hey, I don't wanna fuck nobody up the butt," Red says. "I just wanna come in her mouth."

"Okay, a hundred for the two of you. Blondie up the butt, Red in her face. Deal?"

They dig through their wallets. "All we got is ninety. Can she do it for ninety?"

I think for a moment. "Oh, why not," I say, snatching the money out of their hands. "Hop in. You got half an hour. We drive while you fuck. You both have to wear a safe. Tap on the glass when you're done; I'll tap if you're low on time. *Capisce?*"

"Huh?"

"Okay?"

"Oh, yeah. Okay." They clamber into the back of the truck; I get in the front and we roar off. "Hey, there's a mirror in here!" Blondie exclaims. "Kin-ky." He already has his dick out and is spreading your ass cheeks open. You reach for the bag of tricks and shove it into his hand. "Condoms and lube," you say, trying to make your voice sound husky. "Gloves if you use your fingers."

Blondie wriggles into a glove and shoves a rubber on his hard dick. The two of them grope your body; Red is in front of you, sliding a condom on, rubbing his dick in your face, while Blondie massages your ass, spreading your cheeks and clumsily shoving his lubed fingers into your asshole. You grunt, and try to turn it into a sexy moan.

"He ain't no faggot," I say to Macius. "He just wants to butt fuck a girl in the back of a pickup with his buddy jacking off two feet away." Macius snorts and swerves the truck, tossing the passengers into a heap. The men jerk away from each other like they'd been burned. "Good call." I chuckle.

The two men hurry it up now, terrified of any further contact with each other. Blondie flings himself onto your back, guides his dick into your asshole, and shoves it in with one quick motion. You're moaning in earnest now, your asshole stretched wide, invaded, assaulted. Red slaps you in the face with his cock, jerking himself off in front of your mouth. You try to imagine what you look like, how I feel kneeling over you, my hand between my legs, my face in the glass, watching these louts violate your body. Oddly enough, it works. A trickle of wetness dribbles between your legs, and you pull Red's cock deep into your mouth. He shoves himself into your face and comes instantly; Blondie bucks hard into your squirming ass and comes just moments after. He collapses on top of you; his hand brushes Red's knee, and jerks away.

I smile as two more condoms go sailing out the window, and we head back to Polk Street and pull into our side street. "Thanks, lady," Blondie calls as they saunter off. The two men disappear into the street, Red's voice fading into the background, taunting his friend. "Faggot."

I grin out into the street, settle onto the tailgate next to you, and see a figure swaggering over to us. A man in dark clothing . . . oh, shit. It's a cop. Shit, fuck, piss, goddamn.

"Evening, Officer," I say. "Is there something I can help you with?"

He shakes his head. "Come on, ladies, move it along. I know what you're doing. Get the hell out of here."

"I don't understand, Officer. We're just enjoying the evening. Are we parked illegally?"

"Nice try. I could get you for loitering if I wanted. Not to mention public indecency."

I glance down quickly. His dick is hard. "Maybe we can work something out," I say.

He looks around warily. "Pull into that alley," he says under his breath. "I'll meet you there."

I quickly shut you into the truck and climb in front, and we drive into the alley. I open the tailgate, and the cop crawls inside. I shut you in and scramble into the front.

"All right, whore," he says brutally. He flips you onto your stomach, pushes your legs open, and jams his truncheon into your cunt. You gasp as he presses it in, not really fucking you, but twisting and prodding inside. You clutch at the sheet, trying not to cry, trying not to let him see that he's hurting you. You hear his zipper open. "Whore . . . fucking whore . . . spread 'em . . . keep 'em spread . . . cunt . . . whore . . . oh, fuck!" He groans, and you feel a sudden warm spurt on your ass. He yanks the truncheon out of your cunt, wipes it off on the satin sheet, and pounds on the glass. "All right, you two. Get the hell off my beat. And stay off. I'm letting you off with a warning." I dash around to the back to let him out, and he staggers off.

I stick my head inside the truck. "You okay in there?"

"Yeah," you sigh. "Jesus, what an asshole. I hate cops."

I caress your face and kiss you softly on the lips. "That makes two of us, sweetie."

"Three," Macius pipes up.

"All right, then," I say. "I guess we're calling it a night. Home, James."

"I thought it was Jeeves," Macius says as I shut you in. You pull back the curtains and we spin off down the street toward the hotel. I switch the intercom to two-way so we can talk on the way back.

"Hey, perv," Macius says suddenly. "There's someone flagging you down."

"Really? Where?"

"Back there. We just missed him."

"Cop?"

"I don't think so."

"Well, go around the block," I say, winding down the window. "Maybe we can catch him." Macius obeys, and we drive around the block and cruise back up Polk Street. "There he is," Macius says, pointing to a well-dressed man. He seems to be waiting for us. I lean out the window and signal him to follow.

We pull into the side street. I get out of the truck and lean against it, waiting as the man approaches. He is carefully dressed in a double-breasted suit and black shirt, his long dark hair pulled back in a neat ponytail. He is slender, medium tall, good-looking, well-bred, aloof. He has a somewhat wilted bouquet of roses wrapped in green paper dangling from one hand.

He strolls up to the truck. "I've been watching you," he says. "Interesting operation. I assume the glass is one-way?"

I raise my eyebrows, impressed. "Now, what on earth makes you say that?"

"You. The minute you get in the cab, you spin around like the secret of the universe was written in the glass. And you don't look like the kind of woman who'd be that entranced with her own reflection. No offense."

"None taken," I reply. "So what are you doing in this neighborhood? Not that it's any of my business, but you don't look like the Polk Street type."

"I live near here. I was just walking home."

I glance at his attire. "Symphony?"

"Mozart's *Requiem*."

"Any good?" I ask, bored already.

"The performance was lovely," he replies. "The evening was . . . disappointing."

"I see." I nod. "Well, maybe we can help you out. You lookin' for some company?"

"Perhaps. What are you charging, if I may be so vulgar?"

"You certainly may. Twenty-five for French, fifty for regular, seventy-five for Greek. Up to half an hour."

"And may I inspect the . . . merchandise?"

I walk to the back of the truck and open the tailgate. "Okay, Jerusalem. Pretty yourself up for the nice man."

You scramble to tidy yourself up, fluffing your ratted hair, wiping your smeared eyeliner, tucking your legs and thrusting out your breasts in a bad imitation of a cheesecake model. The stranger looks you up and down, measuring, judging. You seem to remind him of someone. He finishes his appraisal and beckons me over. "Anything I want, for as long as I wanted it. How much would that be?"

"Depends," I say, somewhat taken aback. "What do you mean by anything?"

"I mean . . . anything."

I look him over quickly, sizing up his intentions and his wallet. "Three hundred."

"That's a lot for the back of a truck. It's not exactly the Ritz."

"It seems to be what you want."

"No," he shrugs. "Not what I want. Just what's available at the moment. Two hundred."

I think it over for a moment. "Okay. Two hundred . . . but a two-hour limit. Plus ten bucks for gas."

He smiles and shakes his head. "Whatever," he says as he pulls out his wallet. He counts out eleven twenties and hands them to me. "Keep the change," he says, and starts to move to-ward the back of the truck. I stop him, putting my hand on his chest.

"One thing," I say. "There's a limit on 'anything.' You

don't get to do any serious permanent shit. If you try to, if I even think you're about to, then we will pull off into a nice dark alley in India Basin, and I will shoot you very, very dead. Understand?"

He nods, amused. "Sure. That's fine. I wasn't planning to anyway."

I walk to the back of the truck and whisper in your ear. "I assume you heard that. This guy gets anything he wants. No arguments, understand? Don't worry; I'll be watching carefully."

"Yeah, I bet you will." You pout. "You're drooling already. He probably wants to fuck me up the butt while I sing the *Hallelujah* chorus."

"Well, if he does, then you start singin', honey." I beckon to the stranger, and he crawls gracefully into the back of the truck. "Have fun, you two," I chirp. I slam the tailgate shut, scramble into the cab, and press my nose to the glass. I don't want to miss a minute of this one.

The stranger draws the curtains closed as the truck pulls into the street. Unexpectedly, he gathers you into his arms and begins to caress your body, lightly, softly, expertly. "Shhhh," he says as he unfastens your bustier. "It's been a rough night, hasn't it?" He slowly strips you down, freeing you from your tight clothing. You curl up in his arms and begin to relax in spite of yourself. The rumbling and swaying and gentle vibration of the truck combine with his touch and his voice, soothing you, wrapping around you like a lullaby.

"Now lie back," he tells you. "Fold your hands behind your head." You comply gratefully, stretching your naked body in front of him. "That's right," he says. "Lie back and spread your legs. I know, you've heard it a thousand times. Men are so single-minded . . . aren't we?"

You reach for his dick, and he slaps you lightly across the face. "No," he murmurs. "Not until I tell you. You just stay there and let me touch you." His voice is calm, authoritative, assuming obedience rather than demanding it. It contrasts sharply with the blunt cacophony you're so used to hearing from me. It settles onto your soul like cool water. It also makes your clit begin to twitch.

He spreads your legs a little wider, picks up the bouquet of roses, and begins to stroke you with the velvety blossoms, tickling your nipples, circling your belly button, stroking down one leg and back up the other. The paper rustles between your thighs. He brings the flowers to his mouth, moistening the petals with his breath, and brings them back down onto your torso. You sigh and open your legs greedily. He smiles, and slides the flowers between your legs and over your cunt. "Yes," he says. "That feels nice, doesn't it?"

He sets the bouquet down, sits cross-legged, and pats his thigh. "Over my knee," he tells you. You close your eyes, shiver, and slowly crawl up over his lap, facing me. You look up toward my face and see your own reflection, needy and hungry and high. You shudder and bury your face in the satin sheet.

He strokes your bottom lightly, moving his fingers up and down and around, spreading your thighs apart gently, stroking you up and down your ass crack, over your inner thighs, and back over your cheeks in slow circles. You let out a moan and feel your ass rise in the air, betraying you. "Ah," he says. "There's something you want, isn't there?"

You say nothing. He grips your hair at the back of your neck and twists it. "Isn't there?" A faint trickle of anger leaks out through his cool voice. It seeps into your cunt like lube. "Yes," you whisper.

He lets go of your hair. "Tell me," he says, stroking the surface of your ass, teasing you with his wicked feather touch.

You take a deep breath. "Hurt me," you whimper. "Please."

You can feel him smile. He spreads your legs a little wider, lightly stroking your swollen cunt lips, testing your wetness with a single finger. "Maybe," he says.

You're not used to this. You're used to feeling some ungodly hideous brutal pain slicing through your body within seconds of telling me you want to be hurt. It suddenly occurs to you just how kind to you I really am. This gentle, restrained cruelty is unbearable. You let out a cry of pain and spread your legs open wide, arching your back, thrusting your ass into the air. You forget about dignity, forget about pretending that you don't want him to do this. "Please," you beg. "Please."

He smiles again, lifts you off his lap, and deposits you face-down on the bed of the truck. He spreads your legs and kneels between them. Quietly, deliberately, he peels the paper off the bouquet like a banana peel, exposing the stems, leaving only a small paper handle at the end. He gestures toward me with the roses and gives me a questioning look through the glass, waiting for me to fling the window open and say no.

I say nothing.

He gathers your long tangled hair in one hand, moves it aside, and begins to stroke your back with the bouquet. You feel the thorns scratching lightly against your back, then tapping against you, then tapping harder. You stiffen. Your reaction stirs something inside him; he draws a sharp breath, and brings the roses down onto your back in a vicious lash. You shriek with the slicing pain. "Daddy, he's hurting me!"

I sigh and hit the two-way button on the intercom. "Yes, darlin', I know. You asked him to. Carry on."

He looks up sharply at the sound of my voice, then shrugs and whips the roses down onto your back again. You feel your skin tearing open, feel the blood welling up and trickling down your back. You can hear my heavy breathing through the intercom, coming in sharp gasps, in synch with the slow, ruthless beating of the roses on your back. You howl in disbelief and clutch at your discarded skirt like a life raft, wringing it, tearing at it with your hands and teeth. Tears pour down your face like blood. Your blood drips down your back and soaks into the satin sheet.

The man unzips his fly, dips his fingers into your bloody back, and begins stroking his cock, using your blood for lube. He strokes himself with his left hand and continues whipping you, steadily and savagely, with his right. "Shhhh," he says in the same cool voice. You can hear the anger in it now, clear as glass, white as ice. "Shhhh. Don't cry, baby. It's gonna be okay." You shove the skirt into your mouth and scream into it, sobbing, frantic. His breath becomes shallow, coming in quick, bitter gasps. He clutches the bouquet tightly, the thorns cutting through the paper and into his hand, and comes onto the bloody sheet.

He slumps backward, panting, eyes closed. I signal Macius to stop, and he finds a quiet side street and slows to a halt. I bolt out of the cab and fling the tailgate open. The stranger slides out of the truck, zips his fly, and tosses the bouquet onto your sobbing body. "Thank you," he says quietly. He turns to me and we look at each other. "Thank you," he says again.

I stand there silently, staring, trying to think of a clever comeback. "You're welcome," I say at last. I turn my back on him, crawl into the truck, and shut the door behind us. I take you in my arms, stroking your hair, kissing your wet face, being as gentle as I can with your raw and bleeding back. "Shhhh, baby girl," I say, without a trace of anger. "Shhhh. It's okay. Daddy's here." You bury your face in my lap and weep like a spring downpour.

I tap on the glass.

"Home, James."

Afterword

SASHA WATERS,
COCREATOR OF THE
DOCUMENTARY *WHIPPED*

*I*t was summer in New York City, the early 1990s, and I was living on the Lower East Side of Manhattan with a boyfriend, The Dave, in a sprawling dump of a loft apartment on Rivington Street. This was well before the neighborhood experienced a renaissance, before the hipsters with their galleries, boutiques, and tiny, expensive restaurants serving tiny, expensive entrées dominated the scene. Back then, Rivington Street was home to one scuzzy-looking punk rock club, a matzoh factory, and several Dominican groceries, and that was about it. Still, The Dave and I, a struggling would-be rock star and a struggling artist-slash-waitress, respectively, could not afford to live there. And it was our poverty that directly led to my meeting my first dominatrix.

She wasn't a dominatrix when we met. She was a college student named Jane and the girlfriend of one of the many rock-and-roll dudes, friends of The Dave's, who sporadically came to live with us to help pay the rent. Jane spent a lot of time at our place, blowing off classes at NYU, complaining (along with me) about her crappy waitress job, preparing for auditions because, of course, she was an aspiring actress. A few months after we met, Jane quit her restaurant job and became a topless dancer—a move her boyfriend, the guitar-player dude, thought was very cool. A few months later, Jane traded in her dancing pole for a leather corset and a crop and began calling herself Mistress Jacqueline. She would return to our dumpy loft after an evening at "the dungeon" with tales of a mysterious, sexual underworld the likes of which I had no clue whatsoever. She would say things like "you know when you've been spanking big hairy men all day how tired your arm gets?" Ummm, *no*, actually, I did *not know* how tired your arm gets! I did not know a thing about spanking people for money, about "tops" and "bottoms," about "vanilla sex," or the proper way to whip someone on the back (steer clear of the kidneys), or that there were men who liked to kiss and lick stinky feet. And I grew up in New York City! And went to art school! How had this entire realm of drama and desire, of performance and sensuality and sleaze eluded me?

During this same period of time, I had begun interning for a documentary filmmaker I deeply admired, Barbara Kopple (*Harlan County U.S.A., American Dream*), whose compelling portraits of American labor in the 1970s and 1980s had garnered her two Academy Awards for Best Documentary (the only woman and only director ever to win twice in that category). It was at Kopple's production company that I became friends with my codirector Iana Porter, and it was our shared love of documentary, plus our fascination with Jane's metamorphosis into Mistress Jacqueline, that started us on the path toward what would eventually become *Whipped*, an intimate portrait of three New York women, professional dominatrixes, and their clients, lovers, slaves, and friends.

In the beginning, we had energy, enthusiasm, incredible naïveté, and little else. We had no money, yet we committed ourselves to shooting on pricey 16mm film instead of crappy-looking Hi-8 video (this was before digital video revolutionized documentary production). And despite our backgrounds in film and our personal connection to Mistress Jacqueline, we honestly had little idea how or where to begin. Jane/Jacqueline halfheartedly consented to an on-camera interview, but refused to introduce us to her coworkers or clients, citing their privacy. We knew we couldn't just show up at Paddles or The Vault, two legendary downtown S&M clubs, and hand out business cards. And neither of us was prepared to go behind-the-scenes for a first-person perspective to document becoming a dominatrix for the sake of the film—although we would come perilously close to crossing this line on more than one occasion in the future. Desperate, we did something that, looking back from the perspective of the married-with-children professional thirty-something squares we are today, seems ludicrous and quite possibly dangerous: We placed an ad on the back page of the *Village Voice* seeking not dominatrixes but their clients, for one-on-one interviews—no cameras, no tape recorders—for "research" purposes only. We reasoned that the submissive men who seek out their services, more so than the doms themselves, might be willing to talk.

And talk they did! Men arrived at our doorsteps or met us for coffee with briefcases full of shocking self-portraits; they shared their love of caning/cock rings/verbal humiliation/bondage/fill-in-the-fetish-blank in excruciating detail. They mostly freaked us out. But then we met Marco, the wry, self-aware, damaged romantic who appears in *Whipped*, client and friend of Roni/Mistress Sonja Blaze. Marco, with his ex-junkie intensity, million-year-old black leather jacket, and sheer verbosity, introduced us to many people and places of the pro S&M scene, but more important, to the complexity of the self-described "slave's" psychoemotional life. In the stories he shared about his troubled childhood and his anguish over multiple unrequited love relationships with multiple mistresses (Roni/Sonja included), Marco made us realize how much work we had to do, as filmmakers, to build trusting relationships with our prospective documentary characters if we wanted them to open up before the camera.

So much of what *Whipped* is about is trust, risk, and personal boundaries—not just in the individual revelation of sexual desire, but also in the mapping of that desire up against and beyond the limits of fear, shame, and social convention. The film strives to embody that incredibly basic human drive—not sex necessarily, but the quest for intimacy that is paradoxically made more true and real for some people by the fact of being bought and paid for. *Whipped* is at the same time about the mundane particulars of sex work in Manhattan in the 1990s as practiced by a few charismatic, articulate women, and although, as I said, Iana and I didn't know much when we started, we did outline our ideas, ideals, and assumptions, and develop a few basic principles of our narrative and aesthetic approach early on. We knew we wanted *Whipped* to be an essentially feminist undertaking, in that it would explore issues of power and control in female sexuality without resorting to a cheap thrills exposé, and without presenting the women as victims of men or society. We were interested in women who used their sexuality as a tool to gain power and self-confidence and in discovering why some women would choose to work in the sex industry. And yet despite our expanding circle of contacts in the S&M scene, the question remained: How could we learn more about what it was *really* like to be a professional dominatrix from the point of view of the women themselves? How to gain the trust of these women in order to break through their cultivated mistress personae to the human beings underneath? The answer (in part): Pretend to work as "mistresses in training."

It took considerable begging, pleading, and finagling, but Iana and I finally, somehow, convinced one of the downtown dungeon owners to let us spend several evenings hanging out with the doms and sitting in on some of their S&M sessions with clients. The catch, for us, was that we had to pretend to be mistresses in training—that is, the real dominatrixes would know that we were in fact documentary filmmakers doing research, but the clients would be told that we were sitting in on the sessions as observers so we could learn how to become pro doms ourselves. Much like "trailing" a more experienced waiter in the restaurant business, it made sense that this was how it was done. After all, a person probably could not just walk into a candlelit room knowing how to swaddle a large near-naked, blindfolded male in Saran Wrap without at least having seen it done once by a professional.

WHIPPED

Lacking the funds for a dearly coveted spending spree at Patricia Field, Iana and I—or Mistress Clara and Mistress Eugenia, as we dubbed our new undercover mistress selves—had to make do with clothing and accessories already on hand, which for me meant eight-year-old gold lamé heels last donned for my senior prom, paired with a too-tight black minidress made of a weird, stretchy almost spongy kind of material, plus copious dark red lipstick. Iana, I mean Mistress Clara, wore something equally hilarious and borderline plausible. As dolled up as we were, it is unlikely we could have succeeded as dominatrixes except maybe in Alaska or Wyoming or some other remote outpost where the ratio of men to women is ten to one. The submissive male clients, however, seemed genuinely not to care how we looked, and were quite possibly further inflamed by the presence of an unexpected third party in the room. Silent and aiming to project an aura of severity, we teetered (in stilettos) that much closer to the heart of our documentary subject.

Our dominatrix charade allowed Iana and me to connect in a low-key, socializing, just-us-girls-hanging-out kind of way with several women in the professional S&M world. We learned that underlying the mystique of this kind of sex work, beyond all the required confidentiality and secrecy, the masks and stage names and elaborate costuming, there is a great deal that is merely humdrum. We spent hours with the pro doms in between clients on slow nights, hearing about the most elaborate or unusual requests they had ever heard (or granted), painting our nails and ordering in pizza or chicken fingers. In this respect, professional domination is a job like any other, a business that requires advertising and promotion and security and supplies (especially cleaning supplies).

For all its flexible hours and cool clothes, sex work is very much a service industry, and so it follows that women, the main attraction, do most of the (ahem) grunt work. As is the case in the "regular" world of small business, most sex industry establishments are owned and operated by men. However, in keeping with our wish to focus our film on the experiences of independent women, we decided to follow three dominatrixes—Mistresses Sonja, Carrie, and Ava—who own their own businesses: Arena Blaze, a new dungeon-on-the-block run by Carrie and Sonja, and Taurel Enterprises, operated by Ava Taurel, a "company" (not a dungeon, says Ava) that specializes in "fantasy role-play" from a "therapeutic" perspective.

Mistress Ava intrigued us because, unlike many of the women we had met, she was fast approaching fifty—not an age one often associates with leather hot pants. Named Mistress of the Year at the Dressing for Pleasure Gala—a weekend-long convention at a New Jersey hotel for sadists, masochists, dominants, submissives, B&D (bondage and discipline) enthusiasts, and the like—Ava was the first older woman we encountered who was still working as a dominatrix. She had been in the business for over fifteen years and was renowned in the fetish community for her big personality and Norwegian accent, as well as her lectures and workshops, like the one we filmed entitled "Become a Dominatrix for Fun, Love or Profit" sponsored by the Learning Annex. Geared toward the general public, this half-day-long seminar aimed at bringing a lighthearted, playful approach to S&M to the masses—mainly middle-aged women looking to spice up their sex life with a current partner or learn a few tricks to try on a new lover. Ava also had a master's degree in human sexuality and health education and offered psychosexual counseling for couples through her "company." By expanding the repertoire of her skills and services, Ava had figured out a way to use her years as an advantage rather than a detriment in a profession that, like so many populated by women, prizes youth and beauty over age and experience.

Therapeutic dominance, instructional bondage workshops, foot fetishist conventions (note: do not attend wearing open-toed sandals unless you want a *lot* of attention)—Iana and I were immersed in a world broader, more diverse, more accommodating of sexual variegation than we ever imagined. Going into this project, we believed we would learn something definitive about the whys and wherefores of a distinct manifestation of human sexuality, a largely Western manifestation—the vast majority of S&M culture, clubs, literature, and activity appear to take place in the Anglo-Saxon world. What we ended up learning, and what we were able to include in the film, was but a narrow slice of a community of people from all walks of life, some affiliated by virtue of their shared alienation from and by mainstream sexual "norms," others just looking to try something different for an evening or a weekend.

During the course of making *Whipped*, the question most frequently posed by friends and acquaintances was "So why are you making a film about this subject?" And when we replied with our story of being inspired by the experiences of our friend Jane/Mistress Jacqueline or our interest in exploring the issue of how women understand and use power, the response would invariably be "No, why are you *really* making a film about *this* subject?" (Nudge, nudge, wink, wink.) It's funny because we know lots of documentarians and we have made other films on other subjects ourselves, and yet never have we heard anyone insist that this filmmaker must secretly want to be a black basketball star, or that filmmaker must *really want* to live in a trailer in Appalachia. There seems to be something about two women making a film about other women who work as dominatrixes that raises eyebrows no matter what we say. Were we surreptitiously exploring our own deviant dreams? Living out vicarious erotic fantasies from behind the cinematic apparatus? No, I don't think so. I think we were two young women recently out of school, trying to figure out for ourselves how some young women acquire power, self-confidence, economic independence, and a measure of control over their professional lives, because these things were important to us and yet we didn't understand how to achieve them. And how did sexuality play into all that? The central question of *Whipped*, never directly stated in the film but informing it throughout, is: Is it possible in a patriarchal society for women to use their sexuality as a legitimate means of empowerment? We never fully discovered the answer, because ultimately, I think, it's not for us or our film to determine whether someone else's experience of empowerment is authentic or meaningful. But the question was, and still is, one worth asking, and we hope *Whipped* asks it in an interesting and compelling way.

Finally, as for lessons learned, in the very first interview we filmed, which was in fact with Jane/Mistress Jacqueline, although she did not make it into the final edit, she commented, "When you act self-confident, you feel self-confident, and when you feel self-confident, you *are* self-confident." Meaning that, in the beginning, pretending is enough to make it real, because people respond as if you are not pretending. Looking back at our younger selves, at two young women who believed they lacked confidence yet who "pretended" they knew what they were doing and plunged headlong into the making of this film anyway, I think Mistress J was absolutely right.

Glossary

Baby pizza cutter tool. A descriptive way of referring to a neural pinwheel, a tool used by diagnosticians to assess patients' ability to feel along nerve pathways. A domme uses it for sensation play because it features a wheel of small spikes that can be rolled across the skin.

BDSM. Short for "bondage and discipline, dominance and submission, sadism and masochism," the most common types of play explored in *Whipped!* This acronym is more commonly used now than the shorter SM (or S & M) because it describes a wider range of play and because not all people who are "into S & M" actually partake of sadist and masochist play, the erotic enjoyment of giving or receiving pain or intense sensation.

Many prefer more sensual or role-play-focused activities, or combine a range of possible types of play. In the definition above, "discipline" usually means spanking, flogging, whipping, etc., but can also refer to other types of punishment.

Dom, domme. Short for "dominant" or "domina." In BDSM and role-playing, the person who seems to be in charge of the erotic scene (although the submissive usually shares control of the outcome via prenegotiated agreements and a safe word). "Pro domme" refers to a woman who engages in BDSM play for a fee. Also known as the *top*.

Dungeon. A location designed and decorated for BDSM play, often with specialized furniture for bondage and a medieval, manorial, or techno look. Many pro dommes term their working space a "dungeon," but lifestyle (nonprofessional) players may also design a room to facilitate BDSM play.

Eros Tek. A type of electrostimulation toy. Electrostim involves either delivering controlled shocks or controlling muscle contraction and relaxation by use of electrodes.

Munch. A gathering for people who want to meet potential play partners and others who share an interest in BDSM play. Usually a brunch or lunchtime event held in a public place such as a restaurant. People in search of their local BDSM organizations can look for this term in classified ads; seeking partners from a group is generally safer than responding to an ad from an unknown individual.

Play party. A group gathering (often private, though sometimes open to the public) where attendees can engage in BDSM play, sometimes with people they meet onsite. May be held in a dungeon that is permanently designed for play, or in a rented room in a hotel or other public venue that is decorated for the party and then vacated. See also *dungeon* and *safe word*.

Prince Albert. A male genital piercing in which a ring is permanently inserted and worn in the head of the penis.

Safe word or safeword. A word or phrase that can be used by the submissive or the dominant to slow or stop a BDSM scene. Often the safe word is "red" (as in the kid's game Red Light, Green Light), but any word can be used. A diabolical dominant may choose a word that's hard to remember or pronounce, like "aspidistra." At a play party the public safe word is usually "safe word," and if a participant calls it, others will come to their assistance—an excellent reason to play in public in the first place, especially if one does not know one's play partner well.

St. Andrew's cross. An X-shaped piece of bondage furniture that either bolts to the wall or is affixed to a stable base so that a bottom may be safely tied to it. It often has eyebolts or other bondage-facilitating hardware attached.

Sub. Short for "submissive," also known as the *bottom*. In BDSM play, the partner who is under the dominant's control and is put into bondage and/or flogged and/or made to serve the domme (among other possible types of play).

Switch. A person who may choose to play either top or bottom roles, depending on mood or preference.

Ultraviolet wand. A toy that uses high-volt, low-amperage electrical energy to generate mild electric shock. Wands are popular partly because they emit violet-colored light, which looks very dramatic in a dimly lit dungeon.

About the Authors

$\mathcal{C}$HARLIE ANDERS wishes she lived in the DC Universe, where Lex Luthor is president. Charlie is the author of the novel *Choir Boy*, coming March 2005 from Soft Skull Press. Her writing has appeared in *Punk Planet*, Salon.com, the *SF Bay Guardian*, ZYZZYVA, *Watchword*, *Kitchen Sink*, and *Tikkun*, plus the anthologies *Bottoms Up*; *I Do/I Don't*; *That's Revolting!*; *Love Under Foot*; *Peep Show, Vol. 1*; *It's All Good*; *Pills, Chills, Thrills & Heartache*; and *Pinned Down by Pronouns*. She's the publisher of *other* (http://www.othermag.org), the magazine of pop culture and politics for the new outcasts.

$\mathcal{V}$IOLET BLUE is a best-selling author and editor, a female porn expert, and pro-porn pundit, and has been a published sex columnist and trained professional sex educator since 1998. She is the editor of *Sweet Life: Erotic Fantasies for Couples*, *Sweet Life 2: Erotic Fantasies for Couples*, *Taboo: Forbidden Fantasies for Couples*, and *Best Sex Writing 2005*, and the author of *The Ultimate Guide to Fellatio*, *The Ultimate Guide to Cunnilingus*, *The Ultimate Guide to Adult Videos*, and *The Ultimate Guide to Sexual Fantasy*. She is assistant guest editor at Fleshbot.com (Gawker Media), and she is not a porn performer. She has been interviewed, featured, and quoted by more magazine, television, and radio outlets than can be listed here; for more information, visit her Web site, tinynibbles.com.

*J*ANE CASSELL is a visual artist; makes narrative, autobiographic paintings; is working on a graphic novel; and creates assemblages. She's also a bisexual, middle-aged feminist, mother, and grandmother who believes labels can give others inspiration. She loves the fact that the question "What is sex?" continues to be an important part of her life, and that the answer to that question is constantly changing! She lives with her husband, their three cats, and too many books in a small apartment in San Francisco.

M. CHRISTIAN is the author of the critically acclaimed and best-selling collections *Dirty Words*, *Speaking Parts*, *The Bachelor Machine*, and the upcoming *Filthy*. He is the editor of *The Burning Pen*, *Guilty Pleasures*, the *Best S/M Erotica* series, *The Mammoth Book of Future Cops*, *The Mammoth Book of Tales of the Road* (with Maxim Jakubowski), and over eighteen other anthologies. His short fiction has appeared in over two hundred books, including *Best American Erotica*, *Best Gay Erotica*, *Best*

Lesbian Erotica, Best Transgendered Erotica, Best Fetish Erotica, Best Bondage Erotica, and, well, you get the idea. He lives in San Francisco and is only some of what that implies. For more info, see his site at www.mchristian.com.

$\mathcal{G}$RETA CHRISTINA is the author of the erotic novella *Bending*, which appeared in the three-novella collection *Three Kinds of Asking for It*, edited by Susie Bright for Simon & Schuster. She is editor of the anthology *Paying for It: A Guide by Sex Workers for Their Clients*. Her writing has appeared in numerous magazines and newspapers, including *Ms.*, *Penthouse*, and the *Skeptical Inquirer*, as well as several anthologies, including *Best American Erotica 2005*. Her influential essay "Are We Having Sex Now or What?" has been reprinted several times and has been studied and cited by scholars and writers throughout the country. She lives in San Francisco with her wife, Ingrid.

$\mathcal{C}$LÉO DUBOIS is a BDSM educator, ritualist, and maker of the educational/play BDSM docufilms *The Pain Game* and *Tie Me Up!* She has been a member of the San Francisco Leather Scene since the eighties. Her Academy of SM Arts teaches bondage and SM to couples, dominants, and switches, both privately and in regularly held weekend Erotic Dominance Intensives for Women and for Men. She has been published in *Different Loving*, *Sex Tips and Tales from Women Who Dare*, and numerous online articles. She is a columnist for alt.com magazine.

$\mathcal{M}$ISTRESS LEIA FEYHEART is a queer woman and a pro domme. She has degrees in psychology, sociology, and nursing and plans to finish graduate studies in psychology. Besides more than twenty years of work in traditional health care settings, she is an artist and a designer. She has played in the BDSM scene for fifteen years and now builds dungeon furniture, creates toys for BDSM play, and works in leather. She operates Dragons House, a commercial dungeon in the San Francisco North Bay area. In order to return some of the great energy she has received from the BDSM community she volunteers her services to St. James Infirmary. Her personal interests include passions for reading, sailing, rock climbing, belly dancing, and the martial arts.

*J*ESSI HOLHART brings to her writing a long history of sexual exploration and education: member of Outcasts, FIST, and others; founding member of PSSST (Peer Safer Sex Slut Team); and over ten years of professional domination and lifestyle play. She is currently living happily with her wife of thirteen years in Baltimore, Maryland.

*B*IANCA JAMES is a switchy femme fagette caught halfway between San Francisco and Japan. She is a writer, translator, and performer whose stories have appeared in various anthologies, magazines, and Web sites, including *The Best of the Best Meat Erotica*, *Ultimate Lesbian Erotica 2005*, and *Larry Flynt's Barely Legal*. Her first novel, *Star of Persia: A Post-Queer Love Story*, was a finalist in the 2004 Project Queer Lit Competition. Her hobbies include dancing, astrology, high faggotry, and the pursuit of scandal. She can be reached at starofpersia@gmail.com.

*S*HAWNA KENNEY'S memoir, *I Was a Teenage Dominatrix* (Last Gasp), won a Firecracker Alternative Book Award, was later published in the UK and Italy, and has been optioned for film. Her freelance writing and photography have appeared in *Transworld Skateboarding*, *Juxtapoz*, *Herbivore*, *Alternative Press*, *Swindle*, the *Underground Guide to Los Angeles*, and *Surf Skate Snow Girl*, among others. Her latest essays appear in anthologies *Pills, Chills, Thrills & Heartache* (Alyson Books) and *Without a Net: The Female Experience of Growing Up Working Class* (Seal Press). Kenney currently lives in Wilmington, North Carolina, where she teaches creative writing while pursuing her MFA. She can be reached at www.shawnakenney .com.

*L*ILYCAT has been doing "odd" (phone sex, homemaking, set building, videotaping city council meetings . . .) jobs in San Francisco, planning and stage managing events, assisting artists, writing, and other stuff for many years now. You can find some of her stories at insidebay.com, cherrybleeds.com, and other literary Web sites and 'zines, and coming soon, in *Morbid Curiosity Magazine* and the anthology *Chemical Lust*. You can find her at many art events running around with a clipboard and handing out chocolate and hugs.

*M*ARGO LIN has been writing and telling stories her whole life. Her favorites are the ones in which the key to a better life results from the protagonist's experience of pleasure.

*L*ISA MONTANARELLI'S fiction has appeared in *Best American Erotica 2004* and *Best American Erotica 2005* (Simon & Schuster). She is coauthor of *The First Year—Hepatitis C* (Marlowe, 2002) and *Strange But True: San Francisco* and *Strange But True: Chicago* (Globe Pequot, 2005), and has written for *Agence France-Presse*, *San Francisco Bay Guardian*, *Publishers Weekly*, *Art and Antiques*, and *Playboy*.

N. T. MORLEY is the author of seventeen published and forthcoming novels of erotic dominance and submission. Morley's most popular novels include *The Parlor*, *The Limousine*, *The Nightclub*, *The Visitor*, and the trilogies *The Office*, *The Library*, and *The Castle* (two volumes of which are forthcoming). Normally focusing on submissive women, Morley occasionally enjoys the pleasures of writing about dominant females and submissive men—just to keep things interesting. A female dominant novel, *The Mistress*, is currently in progress, and a novel featuring Caroline, the main character of "Double Dipping," is planned. More can be discovered at www.ntmorley.com.

*C*AROL QUEEN went to grad school and got a Ph.D. in sexology so she could impart more realistic detail to her smut. She is a much-published author and editor of erotic fiction, memoir, and cultural commentary, including the Firecracker Alternative Book Award–winning *The Leather Daddy and the Femme*, the Lambda Literary Award–winning *PoMoSexuals*, the FAB Award–nominated *Exhibitionism for the Shy*, and the essay collection *Real Live Nude Girl: Chronicles of Sex-Positive Culture*. For a full bibliography plus more information, visit www.carol queen.com. Carol also directs and cofounded the sex education nonprofit Center for Sex & Culture in San Francisco (www .sexandculture.org).

𝒯HOMAS S. ROCHE's more than three hundred published stories have included work in *Best American Erotica*, *Best New Erotica*, *Mammoth Book of Erotica*, *Naughty Stories*, and *Sweet Life* series, among many others. He currently can be reached at skidroche.com, and updates his Web log regularly at thomas roche.livejournal.com.

𝓛ISABET SARAI has been writing fiction and poetry ever since she learned how to hold a pencil. She is the author of three erotic novels, *Raw Silk*, *Incognito*, and *Ruby's Rules*, and is the coeditor, with S. F. Mayfair, of the anthology *Sacred Exchange*, which explores the spiritual aspects of BDSM relationships. A new collection of her short stories, entitled *Fire*, will be published by Blue Moon Books in 2005. Lisabet also reviews erotic books and films for the Erotica Readers and Writers Association (www.erotica-readers.com) and Sliptongue.com. More information on Lisabet and her writing can be found in Lisabet Sarai's Fantasy Factory (www.lisabetsarai.com).

𝓜ARCY SHEINER is the editor of over ten anthologies of women's erotica, including *Best Women's Erotica 2000–2005* (Cleis). She is also the author of *Sex for the Clueless*, and her memoir *Perfectly Normal: A Mother's Memoir*, is available at www.iUniverse.com or via her Web site, www.marcysheiner .tripod.com. Her fiction and essays have been published in numerous anthologies, most recently *The Essential Hip Mama: Writing from the Cutting Edge of Parenting*, edited by Ariel Gore. She is currently writing a novel based on her experiences in the surreal San Francisco sexual funhouse.

ABOUT THE AUTHORS

*I*LSA STRIX believes in happy endings. She lives in several worlds simultaneously with her most beloved friend, her dog Venus, and many old books. When not researching esoteric truths, she enjoys knitting while watching Frank Capra movies.

*C*ECILIA TAN is the author of several books of kinky erotica, including *Black Feathers* and *The Velderet*, as well as the editor of Circlet Press, Inc. She was honored with the Lifetime Achievement Award by the National Leather Association in 2004. Find out more about her obsessions and passions, including baseball, martial arts, and gourmet food, at www.cecilia-tan.com.